THE
PEOPLE'S
PLAZA

THE PEOPLE'S PLAZA

SIXTY-TWO DAYS
OF NONVIOLENT RESISTANCE

JUSTIN JONES

Vanderbilt University Press
Nashville, Tennessee

Library of Congress Cataloging-in-Publication Data

Names: Jones, Justin, 1995– author.
Title: The People's Plaza : sixty-two days of nonviolent resistance /
    Justin Jones.
Description: Nashville, Tennessee : Vanderbilt University Press, [2022] |
Identifiers: LCCN 2021057724 (print) | LCCN 2021057725 (ebook) | ISBN
    9780826504975 (paperback) | ISBN 9780826504999 (epub) | ISBN
    9780826505002 (pdf)
Subjects: LCSH: Jones, Justin, 1995– author. | Civil rights
    demonstrations—Tennessee—Nashville. | Black lives matter
    movement—Tennessee—Nashville. | Nashville (Tenn)—Politics and
    government—21st century. | LCGFT: Autobiographies.
Classification: LCC F444.N29 B53 2022 (print) | LCC F444.N29 (ebook) |
    DDC 323.1196/073076855—dc23/eng/20211208
LC record available at https://lccn.loc.gov/2021057724
LC ebook record available at https://lccn.loc.gov/2021057725

For Grandma Harriet and Lola Tessie

The way to right wrongs is to turn the light of truth upon them.

IDA B. WELLS

Contents

Foreword

One of the gifts of growing older is the opportunity to both experience something with a younger generation and, at the same time, remember what it was like to learn from similar experiences in your own youth. Over the past decade, I've had the privilege of walking with young people who saw themselves in Trayvon Martin and Michael Brown and decided they had to do something about the injustice that threatens their own lives and the lives of people they love. I have learned from the young women and men who used social media to declare #BlackLivesMatter and filled the streets to insist that things could not continue as they have for so long. I have learned from the high school students who suffered gun violence and decided to challenge the NRA. I've learned from those who took time off school to demand action on climate change, insisting that the world didn't have time to wait for them to complete their educations. They have reminded me of lessons I learned as a high school and college student, and they have challenged me to reconsider how I interpreted the wisdom passed down to us from generations of freedom fighters who learned to stand for justice and truth in their own time.

Justin Jones is one who has both helped me understand the distinct existential challenge of his generation and challenged me to understand what our deepest wells of spiritual and practical wisdom offer in this moment. In many ways, he reminds me of myself at his age—only more as I wish I had been. Reading about his experience with young people in the public square in Nashville reminded me of the passage in Scripture where Jesus drives the money changers from the temple, offering a moral critique of economic injustice. The text in Matthew's gospel says the young people that day recognized Jesus as the One whom the prophets had promised would make justice roll down like waters. But when they rallied in the temple square, celebrating Jesus's prophetic challenge, the authorities in Jerusalem were infuriated.

This memoir of Justin's experience at the People's Plaza in Nashville, Tennessee, is more than a snapshot of a grassroots struggle for justice in 2020. Because of his honesty and integrity in storytelling, it is also a window through which we can understand the spiritual strivings and understandable doubts of a generation. As a pastor and a bishop, I wish every religious leader over thirty would read this text and ask themselves, "What does it mean to shepherd the souls that gathered together in public plazas to struggle for justice in the midst of a pandemic?"

Justin also knows the wisdom of elders and writes powerfully about how he has leaned on their counsel for encouragement and guidance as he has grown through struggle. I wish everyone under thirty who has marched, protested, or joined a local organization working for justice over the past five years would read this story and ask themselves, "Who are the elders speaking into my life? What strength can I gain from their example? What wisdom do I need from their experience?"

When I was young, my father, who was both a pastor and an activist, taught me to read the Bible as a guide for action in the world. Its ancient stories were never just history, and its parables didn't only offer spiritual lessons. The Bible was full of treasures passed down from people who had walked this way before us, who guarded and kept those treasures for all those centuries because they knew we would need them.

In the collection of letters that are gathered at the end of the Bible, an organizer of the early Jesus Movement, Paul, writes to a young man, Timothy, who had become a local leader in the Movement. Paul had mentored Timothy, and he shares advice with him freely. But reading this book reminded me of the exhortation Paul offered Timothy—more important, perhaps, than any of the practical advice he offered about their shared work. "Let no one despise your youth," the elder wrote to his mentee, "but set an example . . . in speech and in conduct."

When Moral Mondays began in Raleigh, North Carolina, in 2013, we immediately recognized the leadership young people had to offer alongside their elders. As the Poor People's Campaign: A National Call for Moral Revival has established coordinating committees across the country in almost every US state, we've tried to practice the same model of co-leadership between experienced elders and engaged young people.

Today's social justice movement needs Paul's wisdom. I often hear people my age wax eloquent about how young people are the leaders of tomorrow, but it's only half true. Young people like Justin are leading us today, inviting us to see things that only they can see and understand the challenges we all face from their unique perspective. We need their leadership, just as they need the wisdom of elders and ancestors who have learned from their own experiences at other times. This book offers our Movements the chance to have an intergenerational conversation about the world we need and how we can get there together. I'm grateful to Justin for it, and I hope you'll do more than read it. I hope you'll help facilitate that conversation in your own community.

REV. DR. WILLIAM J. BARBER II
President, Repairers of the Breach
Co-chair, Poor People's Campaign:
A National Call for Moral Revival

Introduction

The sixty-two days we spent at the Plaza still feel like a blur.

I spent the weeks after we took down our camp trying to keep my mind occupied, hanging out in nature, and trying not to acknowledge the many emotions I had left in that space we named Ida B. Wells Plaza. The concrete, the steps, the railings, the granite—that physical space will forever be transformed in my mind and, I hope, in the minds of other Nashvillians. They are the physical counterparts to trauma, community, celebration, brutality, resistance, power, purpose, arrest, and rest.

The whirlwind of the summer of 2020 has in some ways passed. I still walk around the house singing the songs and chants we wrote, in call-and-response with myself. On calls with friends I laugh at some of the stories from our summer in the Plaza. In many ways it feels like so long ago, and in others the immediacy could not feel more imminent as court dates approach—reminders that the repercussions of our actions persist.

This whole year has been so long and so short. Time may have passed, but I write from the middle of a storm that is upending foundations all around us. The ongoing global pandemic has made 2020 unprecedented in so many ways; the climate is in chaos as wildfires ravage the West Coast; violent white supremacy is resurfacing emboldened; and our democracy is in crisis with a presidential election just weeks away and a regime that suggests uncertainty about a peaceful transition of power. These are times when the news cycle changes in minutes, a refresh of social media brings new impending peril to light, and there is hardly time to process a long-term response.

I thank you, the reader, for this opportunity to process. It is only in sitting down, reflecting in silence, remembering events as recent as the past few months, that I am accepting my need for healing. What will unfold in the following pages is a story still fresh and suppressed in many ways—the wounds are still raw. The consequences of our fight in the People's Plaza continue to reverberate. They are far from over.

May this story tell our truth to the community and to future generations. May it translate into the permission, the mandate, the promise to rise up against injustice at the highest levels of authority when others might try to sweep it and you under the rug. May it inspire the conviction to take those initial steps, perhaps in fear, but with the certainty that each of us is connected to a larger movement, a movement that long precedes our own lifetimes and that others will join after us.

Finally, this is my love letter to those dear ones from the Plaza whom I have come to consider my family. You inspire me. This is my attempt to bear witness to our experience at a flashpoint in the ongoing struggle. Consider it a tender testament and an unapologetic indictment of where we stand today. Hold it as a reminder that the fight continues, regardless of changing laws and changing lawmakers.

I look forward to the day when young people waiting on public pavement to meet with their governor about racial justice are not arrested, when protests against police brutality are not met with more police brutality. For my children and the generations after, this summer's actions at Ida B. Wells Plaza were a promise not to let up in the meantime. A promise that a better world is possible. A promise that we will continue putting our bodies on the line and dedicating every tool available to building that world together.

JUSTIN JONES
October 7, 2020

We've Been Here Before

The spring of 2020 changed a lot of people's lives.

On March 2 and 3, a tornado outbreak decimated the neighborhood I called home in Nashville. Within a month, the COVID-19 pandemic had changed life as we knew it and laid the groundwork for a summer that would change history in Tennessee.

It was a weird time for everyone. Living alone made it even more isolating. After a couple of months in quarantine, I had finally started to adjust as my life took on a new routine—but I was tired of looking at screens, and I looked increasingly forward to daily neighborhood walks with my dog, Denali.

Staying home was a way to protect not only ourselves, but our neighbors and loved ones, especially those who were elderly and immunocompromised. Governors across the United States called for statewide shutdowns, leaving businesses and their workers struggling or out of work. Forty million people found themselves unemployed and seeking government aid, which came in the form of unemployment (for those lucky enough to get it) and a stimulus check for $1,200.

But while the world came to a halt to "flatten the curve," the threat of racist violence endured, and with gatherings, sports, and entertainment venues closed, we all had a lot more time to keep up with events that might have otherwise been missed in our fast-paced grind culture. Before long, our social media timelines of Zoom screenshots, virtual music battles, and photos of pre-COVID life were being flooded with horrific videos of Black people being murdered for simply existing.

In late February, Ahmaud Arbery was jogging in his Georgia neighborhood when a mob of white vigilantes followed him in their truck, claiming that he was a suspect. They shot him. It was caught on video, and that video went viral. In March, Breonna Taylor was shot by police in her own apartment in Louisville, Kentucky. And on May 25, another graphic video, one that would shift popular American life, spread over every media outlet in the country: a Black man, a father, with his head on the pavement and a knee on his neck, being murdered over the course of almost nine excruciating minutes by a white Minneapolis police officer in broad daylight.

Like many, when I first saw the George Floyd video my first thought was of Eric Garner, another unarmed father killed in the same fashion—choked to death while pleading with the officer, "I can't breathe." Historically, this type of execution has a name: lynching. Eric Garner and George Floyd were suffocated to death. With his airway being crushed, Floyd died calling out for his mother, unable to breathe not because of the coronavirus, but because of the deep-rooted pandemic of racism.

The video sent a new ripple through Americans' consciousness of racial justice—a ripple that had been dormant for years in the majority of the population. All across the nation, people sought action that was more than symbolic. The people of

Minneapolis, where George Floyd was murdered, took to the streets, outraged by the reality that these lynchings had become routine. A call arose from the grassroots to defund the police— an unfiltered policy demand to stop communities of color from being forced to subsidize the very systems that we saw murder our people day after day.

I got a call from Rev. Venita Lewis, a forty-year veteran of the NAACP who was organizing a mass rally outside the Tennessee State Capitol in Legislative Plaza. She was an elder at risk of coronavirus, but she told me, "If coronavirus doesn't kill me, the police will. So we got to show up." Hearing her words, the hurt and outrage in her voice, I said without hesitation that I would be there and would help spread the word.

The protest was scheduled for May 30, 2020. It would be a day that changed Nashville.

I remember growing up in the Bay Area when Oscar Grant, a twenty-two-year-old Black man, was murdered by Officer Johannes Mehserle while lying face down at the Fruitvale BART station on New Year's Day in 2009. Even in the progressive hub of local politics that Oakland was known to be, our people were not safe from the police.

My family talked about the video at home and watched the mass protests covered all over the local news. This was the first time I experienced a community standing together in solidarity against police violence, but it would not be the last.

In 2014, I visited my great-grandma Harriet Parks over Thanksgiving break from school at Fisk University in Nashville. Grandma Harriet was my first teacher of love and justice growing up, and one of the strongest humans I have ever known. Her family had left the Jim Crow South and moved to the Southside of Chicago where she grew up and lived until her children were born and she moved to California.

We were watching the news, anticipating the grand jury decision regarding Officer Darren Wilson, who had murdered Mike Brown in Ferguson, Missouri. It was the Monday before Thanksgiving, which was not a good sign. When decisions like this are announced around holidays, it is often meant to weaken the impact and quell negative reactions.

I remember sitting next to Grandma Harriet and carefully watching her reaction to the announcement. We held hands. It hurt to think about all my grandma had seen and experienced—she had told me stories of the dehumanizing segregation she experienced when she would travel to Beaumont, Texas, with her husband—and it hurt more to see that she felt no shock when they announced that the grand jury would not charge the officer.

I looked at my grandma's hand as it rested in mine. We prayed.

The governor of Missouri deployed 2,200 National Guard troops into Ferguson.

By the time May 30 arrived, I was vacillating between anger, sadness, and uncertainty. Most of us had been staying home for months. A trip to the grocery store or waving at neighbors outside had defined the extent of our human interaction. Gatherings, especially large ones, had been out of the question since February or March. I had no idea what or how many people to expect at the protest.

The news continued to broadcast the uprising in Minneapolis, which seemed to grow every night in its size and its wrath. This was not a momentary, one-and-done protest. My prayer, like so many others', was that this would be something different. People across the world were infuriated by the video of

Derek Chauvin murdering George Floyd; taking to the streets with calls to defund the police was the only righteous response.

Rev. Venita had invited me to speak, but even on the morning of the protest I struggled to think of what there was left to say. I didn't feel like eating breakfast, so I took Denali for a walk around the neighborhood and tried to clear my thoughts. It was sunny. It felt like a perfect spring day. A perfect day to march.

I drove to our meeting place at First Baptist Capitol Hill, the historic church right by the Tennessee capitol. This church had been an epicenter and training ground for the Nashville sit-ins during the Civil Rights Movement, and the parallels between then and now were clear.

I arrived early to get parking and pulled up to see a cluster of folks gathered around Rev. Venita, who led the group in chants. It was a multigenerational, multiracial group wearing masks and holding signs that reflected the calls for justice that had overtaken the internet in the past five days:

> Black Lives Matter
> Justice for George Floyd
> Defund the Police

After greeting the old and new faces, it was time to march up the hill to the capitol. We started on the sidewalks but took to the streets as the crowd swelled. Chants pulsated through the growing throng as we continued our journey forward.

> "Whose streets?"
> "Our streets!"
> "Whose city?"
> "Our city!"

We wound upward, the crowd's energy growing with every step, until the capitol came into view. Its massive columns, colossal staircase, and gray, stone-cold ambience did not feel welcoming to the people it was allegedly built to serve.

The capitol was an icy but familiar place for me. It was a classroom where I had learned and grown as an activist, a battleground where government and politics became personal, and a fortress of injustice that I always hoped could be reclaimed as a home for democracy.

I had spent the past seven years organizing there against the many policies that were killing us, like Tennessee's racist voter suppression laws and the decision to deny thousands in our state access to healthcare by rejecting Medicaid expansion. I had met there numerous times with leaders like Speaker Beth Harwell, Lt. Governor Randy McNally, and Republican Majority Leader William Lamberth. I was not always welcome.

The capitol was where I was framed by ousted former speaker Glen Casada (who was later caught sending racist, sexist text messages). It was the first place I was ever arrested—in 2017, during a sit-in for healthcare inside the governor's office. And most infamously, it was the public building whose interior exhibited a massive bust of disgraced Confederate general and KKK grand wizard Nathan Bedford Forrest, a display I had been fighting to remove for years.

We edged closer to the capitol, the "People's House," as the expanding crowd of protesters continued to chant as one.

"Whose house?"
"Our house!"

FIGURE I.I. Tennessee State Capitol with Edward Carmack statue, which was pushed down and cracked open during the May 30, 2020, mass protest prior to the Plaza occupation.

I didn't see any state troopers yet, but the same old statues looked over the massive crowd: Sam Davis—known as a "boy hero" of the Confederacy—and Edward Carmack—a racist politician and newspaper man who publicly instigated lynchings against civil rights activists. Ever since I had started visiting the Tennessee State Capitol, the larger-than-life Carmack statue had stood there, keeping watch. It was the most prominent statue on the capitol grounds, and it was for a man who hardly worked as a legislator. Edward Carmack's notoriety came from his time as a newspaper editor who attempted to incite violence against civil rights leader and journalist Ida B. Wells. How insulting that this man still stood in honor directly in front of Tennessee's People's House.

All the symbols before us, from the capitol itself, built on the backs of the enslaved, to the icons of Southern "heroes" memorialized around its perimeter, were white supremacist monuments to their core.

With the capitol as the backdrop, Edward Carmack looking on, we assembled on Legislative Plaza. The crowd continued to grow. What had started as hundreds soon grew to a couple thousand masked, chanting, sign-brandishing Tennesseans. The turnout was completely unexpected in the midst of the pandemic and with only a few days' notice, but the people were mobilized and bristling. Their energy could not be contained.

Before the speeches began, Rev. Venita got the crowd going with call-and-response chants over the megaphone. Everyone being called up to speak was either clergy or an elected official. At twenty-four years old, I was one of the youngest among them, and I felt the urgency of the moment like many in my generation did that day. There had to be something different about "this time," this incident, this racist police killing. The cycle of trauma and brutality that we knew at an ancestral level had to be disrupted.

But even in that urgency, I was still wracking my brain for what I could say to this gathering of community leaders and these thousands of onlookers. What could I offer?

We were aware that Nashville Mayor John Cooper was present and that he intended to speak. At last, he was called up to address the crowd. I was eager to hear what he had to say, how he would respond to the unchecked violence of police brutality, which we knew in Nashville as well as they did in Minneapolis. Mayor Cooper was the executive over our city's police chief. His statement mattered.

He began by speaking about social distancing, then made a fumbled, general statement about unity. Not once did he mention George Floyd's name. Not once did he say that Black Lives Matter. Not once did he acknowledge the crisis of state-sanctioned police violence against unarmed Black citizens.

All my nervousness washed away. I was no longer anxious about addressing the protesters. I was just angry. The megaphone came to me, and I looked out at what seemed like endless people as far as I could see across Legislative Plaza.

"No Justice!" I shouted.

"No Peace!" they yelled back.

"No Racist!"

"Police!"

"I was asked by many people whether this rally would be a 'peaceful rally,'" I said. "This is a valid question, but we must ask Chief Steve Anderson if it will be a peaceful rally. We must ask the Metro Nashville Police Department if it will be a peaceful rally. Because everywhere we look, the perpetrators of violence and rioting are not unarmed citizens, but the militarized police forces that instigate and escalate violence. Yes, America is on fire in cities around the country, but it is a strange phenomenon to blame the flames and not the spark!

"I have yet to hear anyone accurately name what is causing this death in America: *white supremacist violence*. We have heard over and over again about the importance of voting and using your voice to make a difference. This isn't a surprise, as many of these speakers are politicians. But simply voting against overtly racist politicians will not lead to liberation if it stops there."

The issue was so much deeper than partisan divisions. It was so much more than left or right, Democrat or Republican, but in fact was in the very bones of America's founding. The crisis of systemic racism required a movement analysis and power that operated both in and out of election season.

"As the 2020 general election looms," I continued, "voting out Trump and other overtly racist GOP politicians is key. But white supremacy is in fact bipartisan. In the United States, regardless of the party in control of a city, police brutality is everywhere.

"Nashville is a Democrat-run city, but that had no effect on the officer, Andrew Delke, who murdered Daniel Hambrick a couple years ago—callously shooting him in the head and back multiple times. Minneapolis is a Democrat-run city, but that had no effect on Officer Derek Chauvin murdering George Floyd on the pavement in broad daylight. Focusing on political party without addressing and understanding policy and the violent roots of systemic racism is cosmetic change that merely creates a more palatable form of oppression."

I looked to my left and saw the mayor standing not too far away.

"What will you do to demilitarize MNPD?" I asked from behind the megaphone. "What will you do to defund our police department and reallocate money to social workers, education, community improvement, and crime prevention?"

He refused to look my way. He didn't even glance up from his conversation. I turned to the crowd.

"Raise your hands if you support defunding MNPD!" I said.

Thousands of hands went up in the crowd. In the speaking area where I was standing, among mostly elected officials, hardly any were raised. I turned to the police officers standing to the side of the overflowing crowd as I finished:

"You were put here to 'protect' us, but who protects us from you?"

The crowd had grown into a multiracial, multigenerational ocean of Nashvillians that filled Legislative Plaza from Martin Luther King Jr. Boulevard to Union Street and beyond. The sun was still shining and it wasn't too hot—a rare blessing in Nashville. Everyone was energized.

A group of troopers had come out of the capitol to observe us, but they were hardly visible amid the thousands who had filled the streets, the capitol steps, and the entire area overlooking Legislative Plaza. Behind us, a crowd of people stood up on a raised platform that ascended to the capitol building. They held signs calling out racist policing and injustice, and had a perfect view of the multitude spread before them. Behind them stood the towering statue of Edward Carmack.

As more and more speakers came to the megaphone, the crowd grew restless. It had been a couple of hours since folks had first started showing up, and people were eager to move. I was too. Next steps were being planned in the moment, but the general consensus was to march to the Central Police Precinct nearby, on Korean Veterans Boulevard just off the Eighth Avenue roundabout. Soon we were on the move.

The line of people seemed endless as we headed down Martin Luther King Jr. Boulevard toward the downtown bus station and then turned right toward Broadway. It was a struggle to keep the right pace for thousands of people. I found myself joining friends at the front of the march, balancing not rushing with the urge to reach our destination. This was when I noticed the presence of mostly young protesters flooding into the streets to join us.

We paused and circled in the middle of the intersection of Broadway and Eighth Avenue, with the neon signs of the honky-tonk bars flashing all around us. Broadway is the city's key tourist destination. It caters to those seeking cowboy hats, boots, and booze. Most of the bars are owned by wealthy white million-aires who give campaign donations to racist Republicans—the same businessmen who had been threatening to sue over public health ordinances that sought to limit crowds during the pandemic. This was a place of economic power and escapism from the realities of the injustices all around us. It was an ironic back-drop as our cries for justice ripped through the blaring country music. We stood in the intersection chanting and waving our signs as groups of tourists stopped to watch or heckle. After a few minutes of waiting to allow those at the back to catch up, we continued marching.

Nashville's Central Precinct opened in 2014. The architec-ture is sleek, modern, and unassuming, and features a wall of windows looking down onto Korean Veterans Boulevard. I had passed it many times without ever recognizing what it was. Now it was surrounded by protesters. Hundreds, then thousands of people surrounded the precinct. I had seen nothing like it before in Nashville.

I pressed the button by the door to make a call to those on the inside.

"Hello?"

"Hello," I said. "We're here to speak with Chief Anderson."

"He's not here and not available right now," the operator said.

"Well, there are a lot of people who want to see him and talk about defunding the police."

No response. We continued our assembly, but from that point on, there was no plan.

As more people arrived, the tension, restlessness, and frustration became palpable. Police had started to come out of their parked cars to monitor the crowd. Just a few days prior, the national news had been filled with images of a burning police precinct in Minneapolis—a visible symbol of the community's frustration and an apparent concern for the police.

A few of the other organizers and I huddled and decided on a next move: we would continue marching until we cut off downtown traffic, to send the message that business as usual would not stand anymore. I climbed on top of a police car parked in front of the precinct—the only platform from which to address a crowd that large—to share the plan with the throng.

As I stood above the crowd about to speak, a young man rushed up to the car and broke the front left window. I was shocked. I froze, others cheered. My friend Damaneke Charles came and helped me get down without causing any further damage. We had attended a multitude of tense protests and sit-ins together throughout our time at Fisk University and I always trusted her judgment. Once on the ground, another person rushed up to bust out another window. About a dozen MNPD officers ran forward to push people away. A man in a cowboy hat was now dancing on top of the police car. He was tackled and aggressively dragged off by an officer.

This was the breaking point, an explosion of all the frustration and restlessness that had hung over the crowd since before Mayor Cooper's speech. Thousands now surrounded the officers and the car, and a police officer started pointing his pepper spray and threatening to arrest people. Further conflict was inevitable. The chaos spread. The packed crowd began chanting and shouting. Cops started showing up in larger numbers. Everything continued to escalate.

Our people were upset. They were hurting. In response to this pain and frustration, we were met with the same municipal behavior that had produced these protests in the first place.

A battalion of MNPD officers descended on the scene in riot gear, forming a line in front of the protesters. They had been waiting for this. The officers were covered head to toe with body armor and carried shields and batons, a stark contrast to the unarmed crowd bearing paper signs scrawled with slogans against police brutality.

Our white allies in attendance were asked to come to the front and form a line with their bodies as a buffer between the police and the Black protesters. They did. Some people tried to speak to the officers, to express their frustrations about what was going on. Others continued to chant and call out the absurdity of the level of force we were seeing. I was looking for friends who I had seen in the crowd. Things were accelerating quickly, and I didn't know what was going to happen next.

That was when a group of officers on horseback came riding our way. They meant to use these gigantic animals to push the crowd back. It was terrifying—and it was clear that the horses were afraid, unaccustomed to the chaos they were being spurred into.

"Y'all are going to hurt someone!" I shouted. "This is crazy!"

The officer on the leading horse pushed through the line, blowing his whistle to keep the horses under control and focused. It wasn't working. They couldn't control the animals in such a disorderly space. One of the horses bucked into the crowd. The officers on horseback retreated, but the escalation of the scene was complete. The line of riot police remained, and the crowd was pushing against them. Pepper spray was deployed. People were arrested.

Protesters began moving away from the precinct and started heading back downtown. Some ran. I went through the covered street that bisects Music City Center and found more officers gathering there. I was able to get by them, still trying to figure out what was going on and where the best place to head was. A young Black boy who looked no older than seven, in a red and white basketball jersey, was crying from the effects of the pepper spray. A couple of young women had stopped to comfort him and his father, caressing the child's head as water was poured into his eyes.

"It's okay, baby," one girl assured him.

This was madness. Using pepper spray on a crowd of Nashville residents, some children, during a pandemic that affected our lungs.

I followed the stream of protesters heading back downtown toward the capitol where we had begun. There wasn't any lead— the large body was just flowing. It was still light out. I had been out most of the day and was exhausted and hungry. On the way to my car, I found a group of friends who were heading back to Legislative Plaza to see what was going on there.

A decent crowd of people were waving signs and standing around the capitol. I moved closer to get a better view. That's when I saw the Edward Carmack statue being toppled. It only took two young white boys rocking it back and forth to bring it to the ground.

I cheered. It was beautiful.

The statue's impact sent a reverberation across the Plaza. It was heavy: a metal monument dedicated to white supremacy.

Watching it topple over felt like seeing Goliath fall. All around me, people celebrated. I walked over to see what it looked like up close, as others came up to kick and spit on it. The top had cracked—it was hollow inside. Troopers came out of the capitol from the doorway at the top of the stairs. They stood around the entrance, perhaps in fear that the building would be rushed by protesters.

It was getting dark and my phone was nearly dead, so I decided to go home. My dog was waiting for me. I was sweaty, and my legs were sore.

When I got home, Denali was happy to see me. I poured some water, took off my hat, sat down at the kitchen table, and plugged my phone in to check updates.

Around 9:00 p.m. I started getting texts from friends asking if I was safe and saying that the Old Metro Courthouse was on fire. Videos appeared on my Twitter timeline of the front of the building in flames. Then a local reporter started posting live video of tear gas and flash grenades being deployed by MNPD. It looked like a war zone. People retreated and officers blared orders through a megaphone. They called it an "unlawful assembly."

The tension that had long simmered beneath our community had exploded onto the surface.

2

Lay Your Burdens Down

The day after the rally, a Sunday, I made a point to visit with folks in the community to gain some clarity and ground myself.

The mayor had already set an 8 p.m. curfew. This meant anyone on the street after that time could be subject to arrest. The governor deployed the National Guard. Similar orders went out across the state, including right next door in Murfreesboro, where the governor sent state troopers and National Guard soldiers to aid local police in quelling protests with tear gas and armored vehicles in broad daylight.

This was not a normal response. In many ways it was an unprecedented overreaction that instigated and escalated rather than addressed conflict. The National Guard had been deployed in Nashville to suppress protesters twice before, both in the 1960s—once after Stokely Carmichael's visit and once in the aftermath of the King assassination—always and exclusively around issues of racial justice in our community. They claim it is the "rioting and property damage" they abhor, but it feels deeper than that.

I joined my local church over a livestream service that included a conversation with the pastor, myself, and a friend who serves on Nashville's city council. We discussed what was happening in regard to the protests, unpacked feelings, and talked over next steps.

Then I went to visit Miss Corrine Matthews, an eighty-seven-year-old, lifelong Nashvillian, who had become a sage and elder in my life. During the pandemic, it had become a precious tradition to visit at a distance on her porch or to sit in the backyard where we would share stories, sing spirituals, pray, laugh, and eat her hot-water cornbread. But on this day we talked about the police killings and the riots.

There was pain in Miss Corrine's voice as we discussed what was going on. The murder of Black people at the hands of white police or vigilantes was something she had known many times in her life. With her permission, I recorded some of our conversation about the parallels between the current protests and what happened in the community in 1968 after Dr. Martin Luther King Jr. was assassinated in Memphis.

"Not much different from this," said Miss Corrine. "It's all pain for Black folks."

She spoke about the hurt she saw in the streets after Dr. King was assassinated and how the National Guard and tanks enforced a curfew in Black communities like North Nashville.

"There's no way white folks will ever hear us if we don't do something to get their attention. Usually somebody has to die and folks set things on fire before they can hear us. Usually, they don't hear us and they don't see us."

We discussed how the police and media were already trying to justify George Floyd's death.

"Any reason they can find to kill people," I said.

"Eighty-seven years is a long time to watch these white folks perform over and over again and get away with everything. I'm tired, I'm sick of it, and I hear so many people say how tired they are of this. There has to be a solution. There has to be an answer."

I turned the recorder off.

Our conversations often reminded me of those with Grandma Harriet, who passed in 2017. That day, talking about the protests of the day before and the police response, Miss Corrine and I ended the same way—in prayer.

"Keep your hand in God's hand," she said. And she sent me on my way.

Throughout the day I had been texting friends, processing what had happened after the rally and deciding what to do with the new curfew in place. It was completely ridiculous and revealed a massive disconnect from the reality of what was really going on. The mayor had shifted the focus of the narrative from the destroyed lives of human beings to a damaged building.

We planned to meet back at the capitol before curfew that evening, across the street on Legislative Plaza, to hold up signs bearing George Floyd's name in an attempt to recenter what had brought us out into the streets in the first place. We asked a couple dozen friends to show up. Many were afraid: there was a heightened police presence around the city and National Guard soldiers stood around the capitol to enforce the new orders. We reassured those we invited that this would be a small act of witness, not a large protest.

About an hour before the curfew took effect, I looked up the capitol steps to see state troopers and National Guard troops stationed around the building. The words *overreaction* and *intimidation* came to mind. We gathered on the side of Legislative Plaza farthest from the capitol, under the small trees along

Union Street. When about twenty-five of us had assembled, we circled and began lifting up chants about the racial injustice and police brutality that had brought us out in the first place. We crossed Legislative Plaza toward the capitol but stayed lined up on the Plaza side of Dr. Martin Luther King Jr. Boulevard, which separates the Plaza from the capitol building.

The troopers and guards gathered, as if bracing for the barely two dozen of us to rush the building—which of course was not the plan and never happened. We just sang and chanted.

People started to leave as the curfew approached, but a few of us had committed to stay right until the curfew, and that's what we did. Some of us kneeled to represent the eight and a half minutes Derek Chauvin kneeled on George Floyd's neck.

With about ten minutes until the curfew, a couple of MNPD officers pulled up to make sure we left before the curfew. They stood around watching us, but we knelt until eight o'clock. We left, but we were committed to return.

The capitol was supposed to be the People's House, but surrounded by troopers and soldiers, it looked more like a military fortress. We had to do something to shine light on the issue— an appropriate response to police brutality is not a more visible and militarized police state.

The consensus was to rally the next day, Monday, June 1, on Legislative Plaza, and to invite faith leaders to join us in crossing the street to stand and bear witness at the line of National Guard troops. Some friends from Vanderbilt Divinity School (with whom I had spent the previous year protesting at the same capitol) agreed to help lead the Monday action. Everyone was on edge, but it felt like the right next step. We needed to shift the focus back to racial injustice.

I woke up early, full of anxiety as I went over the action we had planned for the day. After walking to the river near my house with Denali, I called a dear elder and mentor to check in.

Miss Diane Nash has been a source of light and wisdom, a teacher, and a confidante throughout my organizing journey. She is a national civil rights giant—a leader of the Nashville sit-ins and Freedom Rides, and one of the founders of the Student Nonviolent Coordinating Committee. As a daughter and son of Fisk University, we had connected on a number of occasions and had grown closer over the years.

I told her how I was feeling: I felt hesitant and concerned about the days ahead and about the sustained movement as a whole. We talked through it, our generational divide bridged by our shared values and ongoing vision for justice.

Miss Nash's name had been buzzing around town as the aftermath of the fire and destruction at the Old Courthouse dominated local headlines. A historic granite plaque on the building had been destroyed in the protests. This plaque honored a climax in Nashville's civil rights history when Diane Nash confronted then mayor Ben West in front of that very courthouse, following the bombing of Black city councilman and attorney Z. Alexander Looby's house. It was April 1960, amid the sustained sit-ins of Nashville college students. The bombing was an act of retaliation by white supremacists. In response, Diane Nash, Rev. C. T. Vivian, and Bernard Lafayette led thousands in a silent march to the epicenter of city government, where the famous confrontation with Mayor West took place.

As the spokesperson, Diane Nash spoke with the mayor as an equal, and asked him a question rooted in humanity: "Do you feel it is wrong to discriminate against a person solely on the basis of their race or color?"

Something in that moment, captured by news cameras, was disarming. The mayor agreed it was wrong.

Many believe this confrontation was a turning point in the fight against Jim Crow. The mayor agreed to desegregate lunch counters a few weeks later. It was a moment that Nashville prided itself on, and with the historic plaque destroyed, many in the city's establishment and media were up in arms. I asked Miss Nash if she had heard about the plaque. She said she had not.

We exchanged concerns about the dissonance of those in power mourning property but not human lives. I mentioned that local historians and council members had brought up the idea of renaming the public square outside the city government buildings Diane Nash Square.

"I'd rather you name a movement after me," she said.

I had not heard many confirmations aside from the handful of clergy who had agreed to come in their clerical robes or stoles, and the steadfast group of friends who always came through, but soon after we started the pre-rally before the direct action, a couple hundred of us had assembled on Legislative Plaza. A local minister led us in an opening word of grounding and prayer. Another minister and close friend from Divinity School, Pastor Russell Pointer, broke out in song and got the energy of the crowd unified and uplifted.

"Sweet Spirit, Sweet Spirit, take over this place," Russell sang. As he did, I felt I could see some of the anxiety many of us were experiencing visibly leaving the crowd, replaced with a sense of calm.

Finally, it was time.

We gathered in lines of two, with faith leaders at the front to be the first to cross the caution tape that was draped in front of the steps up to the upper level of the Plaza and the capitol. In the spirit of nonviolent direct action, we knew we had to break the boundary.

I walked first, along with Pastor Napoleon Harris and a handful of other faith leaders. Pastor Napoleon wore a long white robe draped with a kente cloth. He later shared with me that he felt like he was a "Levite dressed for battle"—in the garments of the priesthood facing soldiers literally in army and riot gear.

Our power in that moment came from the unity of our voices in action. Russell held the megaphone and led the crowd in "This Little Light of Mine" like I had never heard it sung before. I lifted the caution tape up and crossed the boundary. We had our hands up to show that we were not a threat. We had no idea what their orders were; I wondered if they might charge down to stop us.

Nonetheless, we crossed.

We proceeded up the stairs, singing as loud as we could. As we did so, the National Guard soldiers began picking up their Plexiglas riot shields and lining up in front of us. All I could think to do was continue singing, louder and with ever more conviction.

"I'm gonna let it shine, let it shine, let it shine, let it shine."

Some lawmakers from the Black Caucus walked down to join us as we got to the top, face-to-face with the National Guard holding their shields in formation. A couple of feet behind them were the state troopers, clutching batons.

Reinforcements from the community continued to fill up the stairs at our side, lining up row after row, until eventually people spilled out onto the grass. It was a powerful sight. All fear was gone. More people joined, unarmed yet with deep conviction, and we soon outnumbered the troopers and National

Guard. Walking up those steps, we reclaimed that upper level of the Plaza where Edward Carmack's statue had been toppled.

"Whose House?" somebody chanted.

"Our House!" we all responded.

The sound of collective voices reverberated off the capitol building in rhythm like artillery breaking through the façades of false power.

Many lawmakers had come out to witness what was going on. One of them, Rep. G. A. Hardaway, who serves as the chairman of the Black Caucus and has been a personal mentor over the years, came over and advised me discreetly.

"You must keep the discipline and nonviolence of the group." He gestured toward the capitol. "You all must prove them wrong."

After some of the young organizers had spoken, we invited the lawmakers attending in solidarity to the megaphone. But before sharing the megaphone, in the spirit of democracy, we took a public vote.

"Who supports policies to demilitarize the police in our state?"

A majority of hands went up right away, and those that did not were visible for all to see.

One by one we shared our list of demands in this way and took a vote on each one: police accountability, funding shifts from policing to social services, all the cornerstone points of our movement in the struggle for racial justice. Rather than just letting any politician come up and speak empty platitudes, we required transparency—only those who publicly supported our very basic policy demands were invited up to the megaphone.

This was people-power in action, manifested against the backdrop of state militarism and the structure of entrenched power that sought to keep these very democratic practices out.

Even as the lawmakers spoke, my eyes kept drifting to what was looming behind us. The National Guard still stood in formation. Shields in front. Helmets and protective barriers flipped down over their eyes. The state troopers stood behind them. Batons out. Helmets on. At the ready.

How were we to prove them wrong, when regardless of what we did, they were prepared for war? Were our grief and humanity present in this sacred time and space, as we bared our souls and lifted our voices in song, prayers, and chants?

Soon it was my turn at the megaphone. Still, my gaze kept returning to who was behind us, guarding the capitol. Were they even listening? Were their shields meant for protection, or just a visible and ever-present wall between our separate experiences? I thought about Miss Nash—how she was able to disarm the very defenders of Jim Crow. I thought about our humanity. We could not end like this.

"We are nonviolent, we are peaceful," I said, turning to face the capitol. "And so my question to these National Guards and troopers is: Will you lay your swords and shields down? Will you lay your burdens down? Will you lay your weapons down?"

I did not expect much. I knew they had orders they were meant to follow, but I clung to a sliver of hope that my words might plant seeds in their heads. That they might think about this later.

I turned back to the young people who had overflowed the Plaza to continue my remarks. Then, while I was speaking, people started clapping and cheering. I was confused. I didn't see what was making everyone so gleeful. I turned around to look behind me.

One by one, the members of the National Guard flipped up the barrier on their helmets and dropped their shields. The loud thuds echoed as they hit the ground. Everyone, myself included, was in shock. It was a moment of the Spirit.

The state troopers must have heeded different orders, because they kept their batons ready. But to see the National Guard, many of them young people like ourselves, acting in solidarity filled me with emotion. It was a reminder of some type of humanity at a time when such connections felt fleeting. In that moment, Russell came up once again, and started to sing.

"I'm gonna lay down my sword and shield, down by the riverside, down by the river, down by the riverside."

The crowd joined in.

"Ain't gonna study war no more, ain't gonna study war no more, ain't gonna study war no more . . ."

I had sung this song a multitude of times in church. It is a staple among Black church hymns. But this time, I felt it like I never had before. I understood it differently. Those lines were no longer just words, but a testimony.

"I'm gonna lay down my burdens."

Someone later told us that they knew why Nashville was called Music City based on our protest songs. I think it's because those songs come from the soul, and from the crowd of witnesses and ancestors in those spaces, singing with us, rooting for us, beckoning us forward from burdens to breakthroughs.

3

"Do Not Underestimate Your Opponent"

It's a strange feeling to have a warrant put out for your arrest. It's even stranger to learn about it scrolling through social media.

Just three days after the June 1 rally garnered national media attention for the National Guard troops laying down their shields, I saw a post by a local reporter sharing news about a warrant for my arrest. I didn't know what it was for. My lawyer, Nick Leonardo, hadn't heard anything about it either.

MNPD had filed a criminal warrant for my arrest for "felony aggravated rioting," and accused me of damaging a police car. It was from the protest outside the precinct, when I used the police car as a platform to address the crowd. I had walked on and off without any damage. All of this was video recorded, and there was a multitude of witnesses. It was obvious that these were politically motivated charges from the Metro Nashville Police Department, under the direction of Chief Steve Anderson. Their coordinated attack on activists they perceived to be "leaders" had begun.

• • •

This was not my first warrant. I had had a warrant put out for my arrest in October 2018 after being preemptively removed from a Marsha Blackburn for U.S. Senate campaign rally. I was booked at the jail and then ordered to be released by the judicial commissioner, who could not find cause for me to have been arrested in the first place.

That did not stop the police and District Attorney Glenn Funk's office from going to another, more "police friendly" judge and getting a new arrest warrant later that month. Officers were dispatched to my house around 9 p.m. to make an arrest. I was away visiting a friend, so I learned about it later from my upstairs neighbor, Miss Ruth Reeves. The next day after class, I went with a group of friends and professors to turn myself in. I was booked on Halloween night.

Rather than waiting for the police to come to my house again this time, I decided to turn myself in to show that I had nothing to hide or run from. I asked Miss Ruth to watch Denali, and asked Ellen McPherson to come pick me up and drive me to jail.

"Sister-Grandma Ellen," as I affectionately call her, is a seventy-nine-year-old retired nurse practitioner, a grandmother, and a beloved comrade in the movement here in Nashville. The first time I was ever arrested, I was with Ellen in a sit-in inside the former governor's office. At the time, she was seventy-five years old. After a few years of trying to convince then governor Bill Haslam to make healthcare available to three hundred thousand Tennesseans through Medicaid expansion, we both felt it was time to join an act of nonviolent civil disobedience. Neither one of us had ever been arrested, but we felt ready after a training session by civil rights leader Rev. William Barber II. The goal was not simply to be arrested, but we were willing to put our bodies on the line with about a dozen other clergy and community members. For many, Medicaid was literally an issue of life or death.

We sat in the governor's office as the building closed. We sat as they told us if we did not leave we would be arrested. And we sat as more troopers came in and repeated the threat of arrest. We sat singing, reading scripture, reading the state constitution, and sharing stories. For me it was a sacred experience. It would be Easter Sunday just a few days later. I never really felt afraid, even as they chose Ellen and myself as the only ones to be arrested and driven to the jail for booking. Coincidentally—or maybe not—Ellen was the oldest in our group and I was the youngest.

I was taken alone by the state troopers. I had never been to jail before, so the routine was still unfamiliar. I just kept singing the whole time: from being arrested, to riding in the back of the police car, to getting to the door of the jail. The whole time. I sang songs Grandma Harriet had taught me, and I prayed for protection.

Before going to the jail to be booked, there is a small windowless room that you enter for the arresting officers to exchange you into the custody of the sheriff's department. It was there while I was praying, feeling alone but empowered, that I looked up and saw Ellen being brought in with her hands cuffed together. She was smiling with the warmest smile, rosy red cheeks, white curly hair, and a presence of compassionate courage. I remember the shock of some of the folks we met, perplexed to see this five-foot-tall grandmother in jail. A state trooper accused her of being "combative." It's a story we laughed about afterward, and we have been bound together ever since.

As I stressed out over this new warrant, Sister-Grandma Ellen offered kind words and comfort. I got waves of phone calls seeking updates and information. I was confused and anxious, but I knew—as I would come to know all the better—that this was one of the tactics of their game: retaliation. We sat in the car in front of my house, waiting for my lawyer to call with an update and next steps before heading to the downtown jail's warrants division. Within the hour Nick called. The warrant was being recalled. I would not have to turn myself in.

Glenn Funk had reviewed the video footage of the incident in question. It was clear that I had not damaged the police vehicle. There was no cause for my arrest. I was relieved, but the whole ordeal still felt surreal. How was the police department able to obtain a warrant contrary to video evidence? It was obvious that a decision had been made in the leadership, and I was not going to let that go.

I was grateful that the truth had been brought to light sooner rather than later, but the ease with which they could make false allegations against me, leading to a warrant for my arrest, unsettled me to my core. The local Fox News affiliate had already run with news of the warrant, insinuating that I was involved in rioting. They placed my photo among others with flames as a backdrop. Sensationalizing at best, racist fearmongering at worst. Their piece was not retracted; it remained up without context or further explanation.

As I lay down for bed that night, my mind was still racing. I thought about activists like Diane Nash, John Lewis, Fannie Lou Hamer, and Rev. James Lawson—people I looked up to who found themselves facing the full power of state violence and repression for refusing to cooperate with the racist, dehumanizing status quo. I thought of elders like Miss Corrine who had been through so much, with so many fewer tools than my generation, and yet persevered.

What I had experienced that day was a consequence that racial justice activists knew too well: the weaponizing of the power of the state. It confirmed what we knew all along, that state-sanctioned violence and the incarceration of Black activists and organizers are the white supremacist system in self-preservation and defense mode. This was the price we had to be willing to pay for unapologetically fighting for our people and our future. Leaving that system in place unchallenged would exact a much greater cost than anything they could do to us in the meantime.

More and more I understood Diane Nash's counsel: "Do not underestimate your opponent."

Over the next few days I talked with friends and other activists about next steps. We could not allow this moment of protest to simply fade back into normalcy like so many times before. All across the country, everything from nonprofits to corporations blasted out "Black Lives Matter" posts and nicely worded diversity and inclusion statements. Hundreds of thousands were taking to the streets all over America, and thousands had been mobilized in Nashville . . . but what would sustained action and pressure look like?

I proposed an idea inspired by the autonomous zones or occupation-style protests that were going on in places like Seattle and Portland in response to the crisis and the protest-connected rise in police violence: we could reclaim the space outside the Tennessee State Capitol, Legislative Plaza, for a full twenty-four hours, curfew or no.

For years, Legislative Plaza had been the place we gathered for rallies, a public forum that sat at the epicenter of state power. It had historical significance as well, as a site of demonstrations during the women's suffrage movement in the early twentieth century and the Black-led civil rights campaigns that took place all around it in the 1960s.

Not only would reclaiming Legislative Plaza be symbolic, it would be practical. That Plaza was a visible space that many of us had become familiar with, and it would bring us face-to-face with the institutions and political decision makers we sought action from. Lawmakers walked through it from their hotels and lofts down the street to get to their offices; they could see us from the capitol balcony, and cars driving by on Martin Luther King Jr. Boulevard would see us as well.

We drafted a flyer graphic, reached out to others, and started planning logistics. None of us put our names or organizations on the flyer for safety concerns, but we did get the word out on our personal social media. People were down to support. I started seeing information about the occupation secondhand through other mutual friends. People were ready for action as the energy sweeping the nation waxed.

Things quickly got weird with an older group of activists in the community. They began to spread the fear that the flyer was made by white supremacists because it listed no organization. They suggested that it was a setup for retaliatory violence. They actively discouraged people from coming.

The only thing I could do was reassure people on social media. Then someone shared my name and number, and I began receiving alarmist text messages and phone calls from some of the people who had initiated the misinformation. At that point, I acknowledged that I was part of the organizing effort, and that it was not being put on by white supremacists. One person still insisted that we not go forward with the occupation because it

FIGURE 3.1. Social media graphic announcing the Plaza occupation under its original name, Free Capitol Hill Tennessee. Around the perimeter are the first demands of the protest. Courtesy of the author.

would antagonize white supremacists—we were naive, young organizers who were not adequately prepared.

Unfortunately, these are sentiments that younger organizers have heard all too often. I have been told countless stories from those who participated in the Civil Rights Movement as students, about how their actions were seen as untimely or unwelcome by those who saw themselves as the gatekeepers of the movement. This was the case with everything from the sit-ins to the Freedom Rides. We celebrate those acts now, but at the time they were seen as extreme, aggressive, and inviting white supremacist violence. Those young activists were often told to slow down, to avoid agitating too much, but they brought urgency and moral clarity about the necessity to act.

Remember that "Black Lives Matter" was once a contentious statement—even for liberals, who saw it as divisive. Now the same groups and elected officials celebrate the painting of those very words on public streets as symbolic gestures. Many of us have been condemned for protests against police brutality in which we shut down streets as a way to halt the normal flow of business as a form of public lamentation. Acts that are dismissed as untimely, disruptive, and even dangerous are often the only tools at our disposal to dramatize the seriousness of the festering injustices we face.

Of course, safety was a concern. I consulted elders like Rev. Venita and other folks who had been involved in security and safety teams for past events. Reassured that we would have people present who could help with safety and other logistics, I felt encouraged to move forward. So we did.

There were other significant logistics to consider as well, even for one twenty-four-hour period: We had to get our hands on camping tents and canopies. We needed to know where the nearest bathroom was located. We had to make sure we had cases of water because of the heat of a Nashville June. We needed food. We needed to know where power outlets were to charge cell phones and run sound systems. We had to make sure we knew where people could park without being towed. We needed musicians and speakers, banners, signs. And we needed to continue getting the word out.

As the day drew closer and the word did in fact get out, the news got picked up by Tennessee politicians like Senator Marsha Blackburn and Governor Bill Lee. They responded with fearmongering. Blackburn actually retweeted the flyer graphic with commentary: "Nashville—radical anarchists are coming to town. Please watch out. These misfits want to turn our city into Seattle." The governor released an official statement warning that autonomous zones "would not be tolerated."

Conservative media pundits began sharing similarly incendiary posts, insinuating that we planned to bring violence, looting, and destruction to the city. This was a line in the sand. If we went ahead, it was increasingly clear that we would be used as an example—a chance for Governor Lee to flex his muscle and win points from the extremists in his base. We could not expect a repeat of June 1, when the soldiers' shields hit the ground.

I didn't know why or what, but in my gut I could feel that this was going to be a different type of protest. The night of June 11, 2020, the night before we began our twenty-four-hour occupation, would be the last night I thought of that space as Legislative Plaza. From that point forward it would be reclaimed in my mind as a space that belonged to every Tennessean: the People's Plaza, not the politicians'.

The Plaza and my life, like the lives of many others who would show up over the next few summer months, were about to be forever changed.

4

Shift Change

I woke up early on Friday, June 12, 2020, prepared to spend a full twenty-four hours occupying the Plaza to make our point. Our demands were simple, printed in black and yellow on an 8×10 flyer:

> Defund the police.
> Demilitarize the police.
> Remove racist statues.
> Fire Chief Anderson.

I found a friend to watch Denali for a day. I dropped him off in the morning and ran errands for last-minute supplies we might need, then I headed to the capitol.

Our protest was set to start at noon. I had planned to get there about an hour before, but I was running a little late. A couple of folks began to text me that they were already there, but many had not arrived yet. Some members of the media also reached out to see if we were still planning on going forward. They were curious what the response from the State would be.

When I got there, a couple dozen people were mingling around. It looked like half of them were familiar faces from the movement and the other half were media crews.

One of the first people I saw was my friend Albert Bender, a well-known Cherokee activist with the American Indian Coalition in Tennessee. We had met a few years before while organizing for Nashville to recognize Indigenous People's Day in place of Columbus Day. It was time to honor Indigenous resistance in a state that was infamous for pushing tribes out. I had invited Albert to be our first speaker and open the occupation. It was important to recognize the history of settler-colonialism if we would ourselves be "occupying" stolen land. We wanted to acknowledge the land that we were on as the ancestral and traditional Lands of the Shawnee, Cherokee, and Yuchi peoples, to recognize who it was stolen from, and to seek permission to move forward. At its root, the settler-colonialism and state violence we face today is the same white supremacist system.

Our numbers were small, so we decided to move to the upper-level Plaza, which is a smaller space. The upper Plaza is up the stone steps and directly at the entrance to the capitol, where the Edward Carmack statue had stood until a week before. This too was significant. We had decided to rename the entire area Ida B. Wells Plaza, in honor of the civil rights activist Carmack had incited violence against—a fitting way to reclaim the space from white supremacist symbols. Someone had even made a banner for us to install there.

We circled up and prepared to march across the street. A member of the Indigenous community led us; as we crossed, he blew a large conch shell. The sound that came out was powerful and steady. It reverberated off the capitol and surrounded us.

There were no barricades at the bottom of the steps this time. We climbed up as one and began occupying the Plaza.

A barricade was set up where the National Guard had been on June 1, blocking us from approaching the doors to the capitol building. About a dozen state troopers stood outside on guard. They radioed other troopers, who soon emerged from the building. By this point, more people had shown up and others continued to trickle in.

As planned, Albert was our first speaker. He grounded us in the history of resistance on the land that we stood on, and talked about the Cherokee Wars that happened here against the settlers. Then he offered us words of solidarity as we began our occupation.

"On behalf of the Native American community here, we support the reclamation of this land for the liberation, the freedom, and justice for all the people of this land," Albert said to the growing crowd that now filled the upper Plaza. "If you'll notice, I'm wearing a t-shirt that says 'Native Lives Matter' and that is to stand with our Black relatives here who are demanding justice in the name of Black Lives Matter. This has been a long struggle . . ."

Other members of Nashville's Indigenous community also came up to offer words and a song as they played drums.

As Stephan WhiteEagle shared a drum song to honor his late father, Lou WhiteEagle, a young white man ran up to disrupt us. He had long gold hair and carried a big American flag in counterprotest. He started shouting that we were "Antifa," and then began chanting "U-S-A!"

People in the crowd watched him in surprise, while Stephan continued to offer his song. A young man, a descendant of those who colonized this land, interrupting a member of our

FIGURE 4.1. June 12, 2020. The first day of the Plaza occupation. Justin stands next to a counterprotester who attempted to drown out those speaking. Photo by Ray Di Pietro.

Indigenous community by shouting about America and how this was his land, was pretty on-brand. It aligned with the very spirit of white supremacy from which we sought to reclaim the space.

I walked over to him to explain the irony of his interruption and to ask that he be respectful as Stephan finished his song. I could smell the alcohol on his breath. I saw the redness in his eyes. He was drunk.

The man said he had heard about the protest and had come to protect his city. Behind him, I noticed some other young white men lingering in the grass, egging him on. The troopers behind the barricades nearby kept close watch—not on them, but on us. I talked to the young man awhile about what we were doing there, and he was surprised to hear that we weren't trying to destroy the building or set it on fire.

"Oh, well, that's what I thought this was," he said. Another one of my friends came up to help calm him down, and after standing around listening to the other speeches awhile he returned to his group and they left.

Other speakers came up and shared words. Other people had brought drums and instruments that summoned the Plaza into a life of its own. Rev. Venita, the resident elder who we would eventually call the Queen Mother of the Plaza, came forward.

We unfurled the banner that we would be placing on the pedestal where the statue of Carmack had stood. It was a simple black banner with the words "IDA B. WELLS PLAZA" painted across it boldly in blue paint. Others stepped up to attach it to the old stone pedestal, and as they did, I could feel the energy pulsate in that space. The drummers started a steady beat, and the crowd followed with the rhythm of a chant in unison saying, "Ida-B-Wells-Plaza-Ida-B-Wells-Plaza . . ." More musically inclined folks started to ad-lib words to the rhythm and another person started to add notes on a saxophone. It was a powerful moment, and in a way, it not only reclaimed but rebaptized the space as Ida B. Wells Plaza.

We started setting up supplies. A food table with snacks and water was unfolded in the center as pizza delivery donations started coming in. We had about four tents and a couple of canopies set up, but no one slept. Everyone was getting to know one another, playing music, and building familiarity in a space that we were trying to make our own. It was beautiful to witness.

Folks used sidewalk chalk on the pavement and posted hand-painted signs onto the barricades. The painted phrases identified why we were there and why we had turned this space into a symbol of our protest. We were founding the community that would come to identify itself as the People's Plaza.

Once everything was set up for the night, we all gathered on the steps to settle in. The crowd was a mix of familiar faces and folks I had never met before. As the hours went on, new people took to the megaphone. They started freestyling and making up new chants, which became the true testament to the creativity of the young people there. I had never heard so many chants created on the spot in a single night in my life. These words would become staples of our movement.

> "The Plaza belongs to the People! We're not gonna
> stop till we're equal!"
> "We want to see Governor Lee. We don't wanna
> fight, we just wanna be free!"
> "Say their names! Which ones? The Police? Defund!"

The chants that first night brought us together and kept us awake through the late hours.

Of all the chants, my favorite that night was the one that helped us keep time. It was a testament to our perseverance in holding the space. Every hour, the state troopers would change shifts. They maintained a presence of about a dozen at that point, and every hour that dozen would go back inside the capitol building and another dozen would come out. For the most part they kept silent watch, but they would occasionally talk to each other, and a few would sometimes speak to us. But the majority stood like statues. When the clock struck the hour and they started to make their way inside, we would start the chant.

"Shift change! Shift change! We still gonna say their names!"

We would keep repeating this until the next shift came outside. The names were of course the same names we had posted on the barricades: unarmed Black people murdered by police that year.

As it got later, the crowd started to thin out. Altogether, probably about twenty-five people stayed all night. Most of us did not know each other at that point. The group was primarily young people, multiracial, some from outside of Nashville. A few of them shared that this was one of the first protests they had ever attended.

I continued to make my way around the space, checking in and keeping an eye out as it got later. The nice thing, for safety's sake, was that we were on the upper Plaza, which was really only accessible by going up the stairs.

Sometime after midnight, two drunk white men made their way up those stairs. One of them was slurring his words and chanting about Trump. He was wearing a shirt for Kid Rock's honky-tonk. He was incredibly belligerent but didn't seem violent. It was clear that he was looking for an argument, and as he got closer to us he became louder. A few of us walked over to stop him at the top of the stairs. The troopers just stood by watching. The drunk friend started getting more aggressive, talking about how this was a free country and making other comments about Trump. They eventually left.

The rest of the night we held the space, chanting and laughing as the hours crept by. Someone eventually brought a large speaker to help us keep the energy up. Periodically a trooper would come down and shine his flashlight over the top of the camping tents to see if anyone was in them—which was apparently the rule we could not break, as it would violate an anti-camping statute. I don't think anybody got much sleep that night. We were running on adrenaline. I know I didn't sleep.

With each other passing hour, I looked east to where the sunrise was supposed to break, waiting for the slightest sign of the sun rising as a testament that we had made it through the night. There was still a fear—even as we tried to relax with music, card games, and laughter—that the troopers could come out and arrest us at any moment. I repeated one of my favorite psalms to myself for reassurance: "My soul waits for the Lord more than those who watch for the morning, more than those who watch for the morning."

The night sky was something to witness. Over the capitol building's silhouette, I could see the stars clearly. The moonlight was radiant. I had never really taken time to just lay and look at the sky. The stillness and darkness that covered us that night made me think about the force of the Universe, so much greater than our opponents (even when they seemed invincible), greater than the governor and the police and the armed state troopers standing around us. There was Something bigger than any of us that we were accountable to and I knew that same Something would guide us.

That first night was probably the longest. Little did we know, it was just the beginning.

5

Power Washing

On the morning of June 13, as I sat at the base of the pedestal where a white supremacist statue once stood, I watched the sun rise and breathed a sigh of relief. The concrete where many of us had ended up was hard and cold, and I could feel the soreness spreading up my back. But I felt peace. It was 5:30. I folded the blanket I had used through the night and checked in with everyone around me.

Folks were in good spirits. Many echoed my sense of relief. We all knew the risk we had taken by staying overnight. We were groggy, but present. People were sitting in a circle laughing, playing card games, and continuing the conversations that had lasted through the night. Everyone's voices were hoarse from chanting, but every hour during the troopers' shift change we chanted the shift change chant.

Because so many people had mobilized over the previous few weeks, our movement had grown and people were seeking ways to support it, even if they couldn't help hold the space in person. To keep the community aware, we decided to share videos over social media to update the public on our situation and let folks at home see how their support was sustaining us. I did a quick video update for social media with one of the volunteers, a mother who worked with a small nonprofit and was coordinating our food table donations. She often served Nashville's houseless residents with food packs and other support downtown. We had connected on Facebook, so I sent her a message to see if she could help organize our food donations.

"We've been out here seventeen hours now, it's a little bit past 5 a.m.," I said. "How are you feeling, sister?"

"I'm feeling wonderful," she said. "I'm feeling a sense of community, accomplishment, and empowerment, and at the same time, humility. Thanks to God, the Universe, Great Spirit, whatever you want to call it for keeping us safe throughout the night."

That was the overwhelming and sustaining energy in the space. We had created a place that lifted up our feelings. Feelings of joy, grief, and resistance. It was a beautiful representation of Tennessee's diversity and our ongoing battle against white supremacist violence.

Throughout the rest of the morning, people continued to drop off donations to our food table. Cases of water, hand sanitizer, and masks were common items. Another young man, Mohamed, came by with a full hot breakfast his family had prepared for demonstrators: hot cardamom tea, fresh fruit, samosas, scrambled eggs, and homemade pastries. Mohamed was a local organizer with the March for Justice. They would be having a large rally for racial justice across the street later that afternoon. Mohamed came to check in and deliver his donations and support.

As the morning wore on, our folks began to trickle out. The majority of those who had spent the night were planning to head home to shower and change clothes for work or other responsibilities. We needed our own shift change. Periodically people passing by would stop to visit and see what was going on or drop off more donations, but no real reinforcements came. Our occupation dwindled down to about ten people. The troopers continued to look on intently, probably thinking we would finally leave.

But it had not been twenty-four hours yet. We remained.

As the sun rose, the heat picked up. Those of us left were drenched in sweat. There was no shade on the upper Plaza, and we were surrounded by cement. We sought a little reprieve chugging bottles of water under handheld umbrellas.

Jay Terry, a fellow organizer and friend from the Divinity School, tried to keep the chants going. With her sleeves rolled up and a megaphone in her hand, Terry (which she goes by) continued speaking to the troopers and all who passed by, lifting up our demands and explaining why we were still there over nineteen hours after we arrived.

Rev. Venita soon showed back up and joined in with a song.

"We ain't tired, we just got started, y'all," she declared on the megaphone. "Woke up this morning with my mind stayed on freedom," she sang, and got others to join in. "Come on choir! Ain't no harm in keeping your mind stayed on freedom!"

We were still hours from noon. Rev. Venita's voice carried across the Plaza, bringing much needed energy and lifting everyone's spirits. Just in time.

Without warning, dozens of state troopers opened the barricade and descended onto the Plaza. The commanding officer was Major Robert Terrell Johnson. He came straight to

FIGURE 5.1. June 13, 2020. Terry attempts to negotiate with troopers after the group was pushed off the upper Plaza. Photo by Ray Di Pietro.

me and Rev. Venita with orders that we must leave and remove our items from the Plaza.

We told Major Johnson we would not be leaving. Nothing had changed, and it had not been twenty-four hours yet. Why were they trying to remove us from the upper Plaza, from the doorstep of the capitol, before the end of our twenty-four-hour demonstration?

"Power washing," he said.

The real reason was the large March for Justice rally set to begin in an hour. They were afraid of the imminent crowd—and afraid that those attending would join us in occupying the Plaza. There were only ten or so of us left; about fifty troopers surrounded us. We were told to move out, and that we would

FIGURE 5.2. June 13, 2020. Confrontation on the grass as state troopers surround and eventually barricade remaining protesters when the upper Plaza and grass are declared closed to prevent others from entering. Photo by Ray Di Pietro.

be allowed to return after the "routine maintenance." Major Johnson told us we had fifteen minutes to move. After that, we would be arrested.

We consulted with each other and received assurance from Major Johnson that we would be allowed back. Then we were escorted to the perimeter of the upper Plaza, onto the grass.

The moment we were on the grass, with troopers standing in front of us, other troopers started picking up our belongings and food donations and bringing them down to the street.

Things escalated quickly. Those who walked down the stairs to the sidewalk to wait were told they would not be allowed back up. New barricades were brought out to block the steps to the upper Plaza.

"What are you doing, Major Johnson?" I said. "We had your word."

He ignored me. The troopers told us we would have to leave even the grassy area, pushing us back even farther. A few troopers tried to physically remove Rev. Venita.

"Get your hands off me," she told them.

There were now two sets of our people, one in each of the grassy margins along the edges of the upper Plaza. We were separated by lines of troopers. Our belongings and donations were being confiscated or just laid on the sidewalk while we watched, helpless.

As we yelled out in protest and continued trying to reason with the troopers, they kept trying to push us back. A standoff ensued on the grass. We knew that if we moved any farther back, we would lose all ground and never be allowed to return to the upper Plaza.

On Rev. Venita's side, our people had already been forcibly escorted down to the sidewalk on street level. On our side, we tried to hold our ground, even with just the few of us left. We were shocked and confused by their deceit after a peaceful night—we knew that what was happening was wrong. Terry continued to chant through the megaphone. Another friend who had shown up, a Vietnam War veteran and grandfather, stood in front of the troopers with his Veterans for Peace flag. More troopers came out of the capitol.

Some men came out to pressure wash for a few minutes. They left as quickly as they had appeared, but we still weren't allowed back onto the Plaza.

"You have to leave," Major Johnson said.

• • •

They kept pushing us down the hill toward the street. Eventually we were forced to the bottom level of the grass. There is a large cement wall there that we would have to jump down from to reach the sidewalk along Martin Luther King Jr. Boulevard, where they had already forced half of us.

The troopers had made a huge mistake. Despite their pressure, we sat down on the wall and refused to leave. Crowds of people on their way to the March for Justice rally stopped to see what was going on. As the crowd of observers grew, more troopers—over a hundred—were brought out in a final push to expel us. None of the troopers had on masks, despite the ongoing pandemic.

I was on the edge of the group perched along the wall. One of the maskless troopers stood directly against my leg staring down at me. This triggered the observing crowd. They started chanting, "Give him six feet! Give him six feet!" The troopers didn't budge.

Mohamed, as an organizer of the March for Justice rally, came to check on us and make sure everything was okay. We were okay, but we weren't moving.

We sat there for the duration of the rally as it unfolded across the street in the lower Plaza. After it ended, people started to gather around us again. Across the street from a rally protesting police violence, they were witnessing real-time police intimidation on behalf of the state. When the troopers brought their barricades out onto the grass and set them up to corral us, the crowd was set off. People started to yell in anger and frustration. The trooper by my side continued to glare down at me.

We had been sitting there for over an hour. People in the crowd started to shout up, "Do y'all need water or snacks?"

They asked the troopers to consider their place in history, to not just blindly follow orders from Governor Lee, and to consider leaving their jobs. A couple more people climbed up the wall to sit with us and hold space. More troopers came out.

It was a blatant display of what was wrong with our system. A public space outside the capitol now looked like it was under military occupation without provocation or reason. They acted like the capitol was under siege, but the only enemy was a small, multiracial group of people assembled outside, nonviolently lifting up demands for racial justice.

Another trooper came down and said we had to move or we would be arrested. All this escalation because they were terrified of more people joining us. Their actions backfired. The activity drew more attention to why we were there, put a light on our occupation, and encouraged others to join. We had planned to stop after twenty-four hours, but their escalation gave us renewed energy and conviction. We decided to remain for another night. We determined not to be driven out by the troopers, but to leave on our own accord.

As it got dark, we lay down on the grass at the feet of troopers. It had been a long day after a long night, and we were tired. The hand-painted *Ida B. Wells Plaza* sign was taped to the cement wall. We spent the night there on the grass and the sidewalk, continuing to hold and occupy the space. The night passed, and the troopers remained outside to keep us off the upper Plaza.

It was then that we decided to move across the street, to the lower Plaza, and make our presence more long term. They had escalated their abuse. We would escalate our resistance.

On the morning of June 14, we moved the People's Plaza across the street.

Another table was set up for food donations, and canopies were set up for shade. We put up more chairs, and designated a

FIGURE 5.3. June 13, 2020. Protesters spend the night on the sidewalk around the capitol as state troopers stand guard after a day of tense standoffs and the first removal of protesters from the upper Plaza. Photo by Ray Di Pietro.

first-aid donation area. Within hours of sunrise, we had already established a sustaining cohort right across the street from where we had been forcefully displaced. It was like the water from the power washing, meant to wash us away, had watered the seed of the community that was to grow here. Our new community stood literally in the shadow of the state power that ignored our humanity.

On one side of Martin Luther King Boulevard was the Tennessee State Capitol building, a stone structure surrounded by stoic troopers in uniform. They looked displeased standing there aimlessly, but fulfilled their role to keep the people away.

On the other side, we had music, mutual aid, and resources to feed meals to anyone who walked by through food donations. And all were welcome. We had more people joining us by the hour, and spirits were high. Many of us were just getting to know each other.

Throughout the day we planned logistics and meal schedules. We made art and freestyled new chants. We laughed and shared stories. We modeled resistance through joy and love for one another, and we were only just beginning. We organized committees since our time there was extending. We needed more food donations, a safety team, and a group to reach out for legal support. Most of us had just been using bathrooms around the area, so we ordered a port-a-potty for the street.

As we set up our occupying community, we learned how to build together and provide for collective needs like portable chargers, coolers for water and energy drinks, and a schedule of three hot meals served throughout the day. New folks came to join us, including some of our houseless neighbors in the area who wanted to support and participate. We came together to make the Plaza an evolving and growing space that modeled, as best we could manage, the type of world we wanted to live in.

If the troopers hadn't deceived us and corralled us like animals, we would have been gone at noon the day before. Now we weren't going anywhere.

6

"Wait in the Plaza, Children"

The next couple days were pretty calm at the Plaza. It was the weekend, so the capitol was empty and tensions were low. We were able to relax a bit, and it seemed like the troopers did as well. They got paid overtime just to stand there and watch us—they would rack up almost $2 million in overtime and travel expenses over the next two months.

We stayed on the lower Plaza opposite the capitol, talking to passersby about why we were protesting. We played music; we served meals. We had a comedy night, discussion groups, and even had an interfaith prayer service that Sunday morning.

We were still ill at ease with the tactics of deceit and force that had been used by the troopers—at Governor Lee's order—to remove people from the upper Plaza under the guise of pressure washing. The troopers had now dragged two metal bike racks to block the steps leading up to the capitol building, and had stationed troopers there to make sure none of us tried to cross. Once again, they were arbitrarily determining what was and was not public space.

In the days since we were forced down from the upper Plaza, I had received messages from faith and community leaders asking how they could support our ongoing occupation. In addition to donations of supplies, we had come up with a plan for faith leaders to once again lead a march to the doorstep of the capitol. There we would lift up our demands for racial justice and seek a meeting with Governor Lee. At least we could try.

We put out the call on social media: we would march on Monday, June 15.

There was a good turnout of clergy, community members, students, and those who had become honorary residents on the Plaza. A few journalists showed up as well.

We huddled up in the Plaza early to discuss the plan, rooted in the philosophy of nonviolent direct action and with the conviction to challenge the unjust, arbitrary rules they kept putting in place to stop protests. Many folks were new, so we introduced ourselves, went over the plan of action, explained the various risks and possible responses by troopers, and went through the chants and songs that we would be using. It was hot. I was wearing a large-brimmed straw gardening hat as cover and a long-sleeved black shirt with a clergy collar. Many of the faith leaders who were helping to lead the action were wearing their stoles, collars, and other vestments to signify their denomination or faith traditions.

Afternoon arrived and people continued to gather in the Plaza while lawmakers were inside for the legislative session. We had a good turnout—a hundred or more were there to join in the direct action. We got in line, two by two, and started to head across the street, just as we had two weeks before. Rev. Stephen Handy, a Methodist pastor from a nearby church, was one of the people leading the line. He said a prayer to ground us before we began. Then we were ready.

Terry had come in a purple suit. She led us in the chant, as everyone joined in.

"The Plaza belongs to the people, and we're not gonna stop till we're equal! The Plaza belongs to the people, and we're not gonna stop till we're equal!"

We moved across the street calmly, unified and determined. The troopers at the bottom of the steps saw us coming and began to tense up. More troopers rushed down as reinforcements and started to get into position.

"Put your hands up so they know we're unarmed," I said to the marchers as we walked over. "If there's violence, it's not on our behalf today."

We approached the troopers, who stood nervously where the bicycle racks blocked the first level of steps.

"Can we come onto the Plaza?" I asked the troopers.

No response.

"Can the People come onto the Plaza?" I asked again to the stoic, unresponsive faces of the troopers.

It was normal business hours on a Monday. There was no public safety reason for the upper Plaza to be closed, aside from the discomfort of the lawmakers inside who didn't want to hear or see us.

A few of us tried to climb over the bike rack after sharing our concerns and nonviolent intentions with the troopers, but we were pushed back. Still no words. They just pushed us away.

We decided to keep moving. If we walked around the capitol to the back side, which was not blocked, we could walk through the grass and get back onto the upper Plaza. As we walked, Rev. Venita started to sing a song that soon became an anthem for our movement. Over the megaphone, to the tune of the Negro spiritual "Wade in the Water," Rev. Venita cried out "Wait, in the Plaza. Wait, in the Plaza, children. Wait, in the Plaza. The People gonna walk onto the Plaza." It sent chills through me.

There was a lot of anxiety and fear about the possible response of the troopers. We had no idea how they would react when we appeared at the back of the capitol. Were they going to charge us? Or were they going to kettle people in to make mass arrests? Everything was so uncertain, but we had discussed the risks ahead of time and accepted whatever outcome there might be. And there was something empowering about the collective song. It reminded us of our connection and deep solidarity to each other. Our connection to our ancestors. Our connection to the Divine. For me, it helped to dissipate the fear. It reminded me that none of us were alone, but that we sang and stood together. That is the spirit that pushed us to keep walking toward the armed battalion of state troopers, together. Our feet moved forward amid the uncertainty of what we faced next, because the songs moved our souls forward.

As we walked around the capitol, it was clear that the troopers had guessed our plans. We filed up the giant set of concrete stairs on the side of the hill and walked around the perimeter to the grass on the upper Plaza. As we approached, dozens of troopers rushed out to form a human wall at the edge of the Plaza. They tried to keep us on the grass with their bodies, but we continued to insist that the People had a right to go onto the Plaza. And we continued to sing.

We slowly moved forward, but they stopped us at the small concrete barrier that surrounds the Plaza. More troopers trickled out of the capitol in the effort to keep us back.

The crowd had grown to a couple hundred people, since more had joined in as we walked over. Folks were chanting, holding signs, all rooted in community solidarity. It was loud and the energy was intense. A few of us at the front stepped up onto the concrete perimeter barrier.

"If you step down, you will be arrested," one of the troopers warned from the Plaza side.

The troopers stood in formation in their brown and green uniforms, many wearing sunglasses. On our side, the clergy stoles, hand-painted signs, and people in regular clothes provided a flood of color. Someone had passed big, freshly cut sunflowers through the crowd. We stood there on the barrier with our hands up for a few minutes. Rev. Venita and the rest of us continued to sing. "Wait, in the Plaza, the people gonna walk onto the Plaza . . ."

Those of us standing on the wall—Terry, Pastor Handy, another friend, and myself—looked at each other and shared the intention to step down onto the Plaza in an act of nonviolent witness and noncompliance with rules we knew were being made up in the moment. Rules that only applied to us.

As we stepped down, the troopers lunged forward to push us back. Terry's foot was on the ground, and a group of troopers started swarming her. As I tried to get to where she was I was knocked to the ground. With my back on the concrete, I couldn't see what was happening around me, but I tried to keep the song going by singing into the megaphone I was holding.

"The people gonna walk onto the Plaza," we sang.

Others who were trying to step down were being pushed away. The troopers lifted me back onto the barrier. With my hat knocked off and a bit disoriented from the fall, I continued to sing.

Terry was deeper in the Plaza.

"Arrest her," I heard one of the troopers say.

Everything became even more chaotic. Terry was knocked down and had a group of troopers pulling at her. They yanked her off the ground and she was taken away in handcuffs. It was the first arrest of the People's Plaza.

While the rest of us were still being pushed back onto the barrier, we started to yell out, "Let her go!" But they were singling her out to make an example.

One of the white protesters asked the troopers blocking him, "Why didn't you arrest me? Because I'm white? We're all doing the same thing."

At this point, it seemed like every trooper in the building was outside. Some lawmakers were also standing on the capitol balcony pointing, laughing, and taking photos. They were all white, and I recognized most of their faces as Republican members. Some of the other lawmakers, primarily from the Black Caucus, had been watching what was going on too. They walked down the capitol steps to join us.

The crowd was still reeling from what they had just witnessed. Terry was now out of sight, having been taken into the building. Many of us were concerned for her safety. We kept yelling to the troopers to let her go and asking where exactly they had taken her. They wouldn't answer. The troopers told us to move back. They were trying to get people to settle down, but we refused to do so. We weren't leaving without Terry.

Eventually, a couple of the lawmakers standing with us were able to negotiate with the troopers' commanding officers and get more information. Terry had not been taken down the street to the jail yet. She was still in the building.

We continued to stand along the perimeter of the upper Plaza, chanting and singing. The lawmakers inside could not ignore what was happening. Many of them had left the meeting inside to see what was going on. The upper Plaza was completely surrounded by people.

It was a while before Terry came out. They were able to reach an agreement for her to be released with a citation. When she came out, everyone cheered. Terry stepped up onto the concrete wall and held up her fist. Strong, resilient, and unmoved. This was the power of the People.

We recongregated on the grass while the troopers stood in their wall formation. Our presence had become an almost celebratory act of resistance. Many people had joined us in solidarity. Rev. Venita continued to lead us in song. Two drummers had come out to play for us, including well-known drummer Darren King. The crowd formed a circle around the drummers while others came forward to speak or lead chants. The drums provided even more rhythm for our songs and echoed around the Plaza. Throughout the large crowd, people held up their sunflowers, long, thick stems waving back and forth, as if they were the banners of our cause.

We were still there on the grass when it got dark.

Around nine o'clock I went home to change my clothes. The day had been long and hot, and I had sweat through everything I was wearing. I felt a sense of peace from the size of the turnout, and felt the movement of the Spirit that guided our action. So many new faces were able to see what was happening in the Plaza—the extreme reaction of the troopers by order of the governor, our collective power, and the need to hold the space.

That night, as I was driving back, I learned that twenty-one arrests had been made among the people who refused to leave the grass. Those arrested were not taken to the jail, but were handcuffed and given citations, primarily for "camping" on state property. The law against camping on state property had been passed by state lawmakers in 2012 in response to the Occupy movement, when people camped on Wall Street, at state capitol buildings, and outside city halls across the nation to call attention to economic inequality.

After receiving the citations and being released that night, people were still not intimidated. They chose to remain. We regrouped and returned to the canopies across the street where we had set up our camp.

The People would continue to wait in the Plaza.

7

Capitol Hill

We were able to hold the space on the lower Plaza across from the capitol without incident that night, but we were still not allowed on the upper Plaza in front of the capitol building.

Meanwhile, up on Capitol Hill, there was a lot of discussion among lawmakers about what had happened the previous day. Questions arose from some of the Democratic members as to why our group in particular was not allowed on the Plaza, why we were arrested for being there, while some others were able to visit as "guests"—even *inside the building* to watch proceedings from the House chamber gallery. Media coverage put a spotlight on what was happening as well. The worse we were treated, the more people came to help.

The next morning, June 16, we were informed by some of the supportive lawmakers that a small number of us would be permitted to go inside the capitol to view the House session in the gallery.

We were allowed a very "limited number" because of "COVID restriction guidelines." The Republican leadership, under House Speaker Cameron Sexton, had failed to take COVID-19 or the public health guidelines seriously. Tennessee still did not have a statewide mask mandate, most counties did not abide by social distancing guidelines, most of the lawmakers didn't wear masks, and our representatives ridiculed other states that had issued shutdown orders as an "overreaction." Using the pandemic to restrict us from gathering in protest was convenient.

Ten people was as high as they would go, though they said the gallery could accommodate twenty-five and still abide by COVID-19 restrictions.

I went in with groups twice that day. It was the last week of the regular legislative session; the Senate and House were mostly wrapping up on passing their bills.

The morning session was my first time back into the capitol rotunda since being arrested and banned from the premises the previous year. I had been arrested at a protest against the Ku Klux Klan monument to Nathan Bedford Forrest in the rotunda, and was falsely accused of assaulting the House Speaker at the time, Glen Casada, with a paper cup of iced tea. Soon after that, Casada and his chief of staff, Cade Cothren, were forced to resign when news surfaced of a false email their office submitted to the district attorney to get my bond revoked—on top of cocaine use, racist comments, and sexist text messages. After that debacle, we reached an agreement with the special prosecutor assigned to my case who decided not to prosecute my charges as long as I abided by my ban from the Capitol Hill grounds for the year.

That year had just ended. It was strange to walk inside the capitol after all that, especially under the circumstances. As soon as we entered we had an escort of troopers who walked us from the metal detectors to the House gallery. This was the first time I had ever seen such a thing in the legislature. The troopers said we could not wait in the rotunda area, where lawmakers passed to enter the chambers. They rushed us up to the gallery where a few of the troopers remained behind us. The morning passed without incident.

We came back that evening for the second half of the day's session. Everything seemed to be routine. We were back in the House gallery with our escort, watching bills being voted on. The bills were going through quickly. The clerk shouted out bill numbers in a loud, fast voice that almost sounded like an auctioneer. There wasn't much discussion or debate. It had been a long day and most representatives were on their phones or tablets.

Then a resolution that seemed straightforward drew the objection of House Republican leader William Lamberth. The resolution was to memorialize a young woman, Ashanti Posey, who had been killed in Nashville at the hands of gun violence. She was a student, basketball player, and community volunteer, on her way to college in the fall.

Representative Lamberth stood up to offer his objection with the House Republican caucus chairman, Jeremy Faison, standing at his side.

"I did some research and looked up exactly what led to this young lady's untimely demise," Lamberth said on the floor. "Due to the behavior and, I would say, choices that she was involved in at the time, I could not in good conscience vote in favor of this."

Lamberth went on to slander this slain young Black teen and talked about a police report that referenced marijuana use. As the Republican majority leader in the House, Lamberth swayed his caucus and they voted against the resolution.

The same lawmakers who fought to protect the bust of a Klan leader and his confederates under the false narrative that those figures "redeemed their actions later in life" refused to pass a simple memorial resolution honoring a recently murdered young Black woman. Instead, they took the opportunity to scandalize her even in death. It was so blatant. Those of us standing in the gallery were shocked.

Right after the vote, Rep. Antonio Parkinson, a Black lawmaker from Memphis, got up out of his seat and started yelling.

"Bullshit!" he screamed as he walked to the center of the aisle of the House floor. "This is bullshit!"

House Speaker Sexton started banging his gavel and shouting out, "You're out of order! You're out of order!"

Those of us in the gallery started clapping. This was the only human response to the evil we had just seen from an almost all-white caucus of Republican legislators.

"No clapping in the gallery!" Speaker Sexton scolded.

The House floor was in chaos with members yelling and the Speaker banging his gavel. Speaker Sexton ordered the Democratic chairman, Mike Stewart, "Restrain your member . . . decorum on the floor does not require profanity."

Rep. Parkinson shouted back at him from the House floor, "Remove me, Mr. Speaker!"

We continued to applaud in the balcony.

"Sergeant-at-arms, remove them from the balcony. No clapping," the Speaker announced as the troopers moved in our direction. This is what they had been waiting for. One by one they grabbed our arms and pulled us away.

We started chanting, "Black Lives Matter! Black Lives Matter! Black Lives Matter!"

I walked away still chanting, with troopers stalking behind me. Another young man who had come to support the Plaza protests was lying face down in front of the doors to exit the gallery. Two troopers were holding his arms behind his back. They lifted and tried to carry him. More troopers were coming up as we walked down the stairs. Even more were at the bottom surrounding the capitol rotunda. Three of us were pointed out to be arrested, and the rest were hurried away and escorted onto the elevators.

"Him, and him, and her. Arrest them," Lieutenant Michael Morgan said, pointing us out as he ordered the other troopers.

They started pulling at us. The young woman, Abby Barrentine, started screaming, afraid and in pain as two large men forced her arms behind her back. She had been silent the entire time we were in the balcony. When Abby joined the Plaza that first night it was her first time ever participating in a protest. This was also her first time being arrested. The troopers got rougher as they tussled to restrain her.

"Stop, you're hurting her!" I yelled. I tried to move closer, but was yanked back.

"Charge him with assault," Lieutenant Morgan said to his fellow troopers. By this time some of the Democratic lawmakers had come out to the commotion, trying to keep the troopers from being so physically aggressive.

"Come on guys, that young lady wasn't even doing anything," I heard one of them say behind me as Abby was dragged away, still crying out.

Abby, myself, and another young man were taken to the basement, and then transported to the "mobile booking unit" down by the football stadium. It's basically a trailer with large dog kennels for people to wait in while being processed. We checked in with each other through the bars. Abby was still visibly shaken. After having our mugshots and fingerprints taken we waited an hour and then were driven down to the Nashville jail for booking. We were brought inside, searched a third time, and held until late that night. This was my first arrest as part of the Plaza protests. It would not be the last.

After being released, we were greeted by friends outside who were helping with legal support to make sure we got out. They shared snacks and shoulders to lean on as we walked back up the street to the Plaza and joined the others who continued to hold the space.

The next day, June 17, the troopers tried a new tactic to end our protests. Dozens of them were deployed out of the capitol building to raid us, confiscating water, canopies, medications, and personal belongings. They also had the port-a-potty we had ordered removed. It was an aggressive escalation meant to intimidate us. Some of them ripped down the signs and community art we had displayed.

However, as they tried to rip down the banner displaying the words *Ida B. Wells Plaza* and bearing her photograph, they were stopped. Dragon, one of our houseless friends who had been part of the protests since the first night, put his body in front of the banner and refused to move. They ordered him to move out of the way, but he stood there with his hands up and refused to comply.

"If you don't move, you will be arrested," the trooper commanded.

"I am your authority. I am the Black Dragon. Take me to jail," Dragon responded, looking the trooper in his eyes. He refused to move. It was the first time since our protests began that I had heard him speak. He stood with power and dignity, with his grayish-black beard and white t-shirt, holding his hands up, and remaining unmovable. Five more troopers came over as backup and surrounded him.

FIGURE 7.1. June 17, 2020. Dragon faces off with line of state troopers on the street in front of the Tennessee State Capitol. Troopers had just raided the Plaza and confiscated people's belongings. Photo by Ray Di Pietro.

"You cannot keep this sign affixed here. It must be removed," the trooper ordered again.

"I will not submit," Dragon replied, resting the back of his head on the sign, arms still raised. "If you got to take me to jail, you gotta do what you got to do. But I refuse." The troopers kept trying to convince him to get out of the way, but Dragon stood firm and repeated again, "I refuse."

The troopers then moved one of their metal bicycle racks in front of him and said that it was now an unauthorized area. As the troopers surrounded him, Sergeant John Grinder got on the phone to seek orders from his superiors about what to do. They continued to threaten Dragon with arrest.

"Where is the law that says he can't stand there?" someone asked them.

"But y'all put that gate there," another man from the house-less community yelled out. "This is how they always treat us."

The standoff continued.

The troopers kept getting closer to Dragon and called for even more backup. They had over a dozen troopers around him and more came out of the building with video cameras.

"This is a solo act. If you're gonna take me to jail, do it. But I'm not moving," Dragon told them.

People on the road could see what was going on and some stopped to watch what was happening. Multiple cameras were recording the interaction. Sergeant Grinder became even more irritated and upset, but after placing a call to his superiors, he and the other troopers backed down and the sign remained up. At least for a couple of hours. When we crossed the street to return to the lower Plaza, two troopers came from behind the barricade and removed it.

Later that day, Ashanti Posey's mom, Amber Posey, also came out to join us and speak to the media in the Plaza. She shared her frustration and hurt at the racist mischaracteriza-tions made by Republican lawmakers the night before when they failed to pass the resolution in memory of her daughter.

Standing across the street from the capitol, wearing a t-shirt with Ashanti's picture on it, Amber Posey declared, "If they want to know the narrative of who Ashanti Posey was, I'd be more than happy to speak with anybody. One person's opinion doesn't define her legacy."

We gathered around her and she thanked the activists who spoke out the night before. After a few more interviews, we fol-lowed her and Ashanti's younger sisters in a procession across the street to the capitol steps where we were stopped by the bicycle racks and the troopers standing guard at the foot of the steps.

Something in that moment released the flood of a mother's grief. Looking at the troopers blocking our way, Miss Posey cried out, "You do this for a check. I do this for my child's story. There's no payroll that will ever stop me from seeking justice. There is no payroll that will ever stop me from telling her story. . . . You will know who I am. And you will know who Ashanti Posey was. Not what the police say. What I say. Because I am the author of her story now. And I will be the only one that tells it. My prayers are with y'all."

All of us standing with her were moved to tears and applause, an outbreak of grief and righteous outrage. This was the power of a mother's witness, and a pain felt much too often at the hands of gun violence and deadly police encounters. Miss Posey took a poster-sized photo of Ashanti that her younger daughters had been holding and taped it to the barricade. At the top they had written the words "Speak her legacy." Many crossed Martin Luther King Jr. Boulevard to offer tearful hugs and gratitude for the family's strength amidst tragedy and the subsequent callousness of lawmakers like Rep. Lamberth. Miss Posey offered to meet with him and even extended an invitation for him to come to their home to learn who Ashanti was. It was an offer of grace in the face of cruelty. A lesson for us all. We returned to the lower Plaza.

The following day, troopers returned once again to raid the Plaza in the middle of the afternoon. They filed out of the capitol building with rubber gloves on, again confiscating water, canopies, coolers, first-aid supplies, and personal belongings. They carelessly threw our items in the back of a large white moving truck. The coolers full of ice and cold drinks spilled over everything as they were slung inside thoughtlessly.

In the midst of the rush, a scuffle occurred and an ambulance was called for a woman who was houseless and trying to hold on to her belongings. An altercation ensued while she was trying to keep her things from the troopers, and she began to have a seizure. The troopers didn't care; they were ordered to confiscate everything and throw it inside the truck. All they knew were orders and how to follow them. They were protected from the consequences.

All of us had been scattered around the Plaza, running with what we could carry and trying to record what was happening with our phones. But at that point we circled around the woman to keep the troopers away until the ambulance arrived so she could receive medical care.

No arrests were made, but the Plaza was pretty much picked clean.

Things only escalated from there. The troopers continued to use war-like tactics against us. They raided at any time of day or night, isolated individuals, yelled out orders, and treated the Plaza like a territory to be conquered.

But each time they raided, we shared the videos of what was happening and put out a call for more items to replace those that had been stolen under command of Governor Lee. Each time, the community showed up with even more canopies, cases of water, meals, masks, and bottles of hand sanitizer.

Rev. Venita made a new chant about it that we started to use regularly: "Y'all take it down, we gon' put it right back, put it right back, put it right back!"

The raids continued.

On Juneteenth, the day celebrating the announcement to the enslaved living in Texas that they had been freed by Abraham

FIGURE 7.2. June 20, 2020. Teens for Equality group hold street signs and dance to support the Plaza occupation. They organized and led some of that summer's largest marches in the community. Photo by Ray Di Pietro.

Lincoln's Emancipation Proclamation, confrontations exploded into a face-to-face standoff that openly transformed the Plaza into an active battleground.

Hundreds of community members had turned out for the occasion, in addition to the dozens that were holding down the occupation. It started as a time of celebration and Black joy as forms of resistance. Music was blasting on large speakers and an electric slide line was lighting up the Plaza. After a while, the gathering organically overflowed to the street, extending from the lower Plaza to the metal bike racks blocking the capitol steps. As we gathered there, more troopers were sent out, and we kneeled in the street and sidewalk facing the capitol and troopers in a moment of silence.

FIGURE 7.3. June 18, 2020. A protester stands in front of the stairs to the upper Plaza. The troopers cited "power washing" and "COVID concerns" as their reasoning for preventing people from accessing the public space. Photo by Ray Di Pietro.

Eventually, we began to march around to the grass on the perimeter of the Plaza, where the last action led by faith leaders had been stopped. The People still wanted to walk onto the Plaza. A battalion of troopers rushed forward to form a wall, this time on the grass area itself. They tried to push three hundred of us back, but were unsuccessful.

National Guard troops were called from inside the building as reinforcements. They had spent the week inside on standby, but they came out now in their military fatigues, helmets, and riot shields to back up the troopers who were pushing up against the crowd. On our side, someone had brought a full-sized Pan-African flag. The red, green, and black stripes waved in the wind as our battle flag on the frontlines. The troopers

FIGURE 7.4. June 19, 2020. Juneteenth standoff with troopers on the grassy perimeter of the upper Plaza. Not too long after this photo was taken, National Guard troops were also deployed from within the capitol. Photo by Ray Di Pietro.

and National Guard tried to force us away, but we held our ground and refused to be pushed back. As the back-and-forth continued, one trooper pepper sprayed a couple of folks around him. It was chaotic.

Finally, to de-escalate, a few of us took a knee at the front of the line. Things were becoming violent. Troopers were aggressively pushing up against people and threatening even greater use of force. As we kneeled, others followed, and soon the image of who the aggressor was became obvious to all those watching on the street. Only one side remained standing. Only one side was literally dressed for war. The question was: Who exactly was being served and protected? And for what?

No arrests were made that night. The troopers took a few steps back, and we returned across the street to the lower Plaza.

Later that evening, we had our first mass meeting on the steps. This would become our main decision-making process moving forward. We called it General Assembly, but unlike the hijacked process in the capitol across the street, we used direct democracy and transparent decision making as a way to keep participants updated as we continued to grow and welcome new folks.

Things were pretty calm for a day or so. Then the troopers resumed their intimidation tactics. A couple of days after the Juneteenth standoff, dozens of troopers were sent out again to remove protest signs. We put them back up and rebuilt. Then the troopers came out again. And the cycle repeated.

On the morning of June 23, conflict once again escalated into a standoff on the grass. A few of us walked around the building to the perimeter of the upper Plaza again, tired of the troopers' continual harassment and aggression. We stood on the grass and remained. Unlike the Juneteenth action when three hundred were gathered, there were probably only a dozen of us. We were met with nearly four times as many troopers.

Over the previous few days, we had seen people walking their dogs and jogging on the capitol grass without any issue. They were not being stopped or told they weren't allowed to walk there. But as soon as we stepped on the grass, about forty troopers descended from the building to form their human wall.

A graduate student who had become a key logistical organizer at the Plaza livestreamed everything.

"The Plaza belongs to the People, and we're not gonna stop till we're equal," the few of us began to chant. One trooper came forward to tell us to leave. We refused to move, and explained the disparity of treatment when other people were allowed on the grass without incident.

"The Plaza belongs to the People, and we're not gonna stop till we're equal," we continued to chant.

We stood there for a couple of hours, chanting and holding ground. The troopers didn't budge and their commander, Major Doug Taylor, seemed uncertain of what to do. They had been making rules arbitrarily, but they did not know how to enforce them when it came to actual policies. So they did what they always did: they threatened to arrest us if we crossed the line.

We stood there, chanting, singing, and looking into the eyes of the troopers before us. We were greatly outnumbered. The morning shifts at the Plaza were the hardest time in terms of numbers. Most people would go home to change clothes after spending the night, but a dozen or so of us always remained. After a while we sat down on the concrete barrier dividing the upper Plaza and the grass.

"How much longer will you ignore us?" Terry asked over the megaphone. I was sitting next to four other protesters. No one on our side was older than twenty-five. We were young people sitting together on public space and facing armed state troopers intent on pushing us away.

We remained.

Major Taylor was on the phone with his superiors, giving updates on what was going on and seeking clarity on orders moving forward. Many of us were bracing for the possibility of arrest. It would be easy for them to swoop down onto our small group and arrest us all. But we stayed.

Major Taylor looked displeased. He seemed to be irritated with his phone conversation. He stood above us, glaring down and glancing away as he talked. Then the unexpected happened. The order was given for troopers to stand down and move back to the capitol building where they had been our first night. We looked at each other in shock.

The troopers began to disperse and walk back up toward the capitol. They removed the barricades blocking the perimeter. Their wall opened and we were able to walk through. In my mind, I could only think of Exodus: the Red Sea parting to make way for the Israelites fleeing Pharaoh's army. We all began to cheer. It had been almost two weeks since we were last able to gather in that space, the upper Plaza, at the doors of the capitol, when they closed it under the guise of "power washing."

"The Plaza belongs to the people, and we're not gonna stop till we're equal," we chanted with new meaning. It was a small victory. But it was also a reclamation of public space and higher ground. We walked onto the upper Plaza cheering and hugging each other, still slightly stunned at what had just occurred.

We brought the Ida B. Wells Plaza banner to hang up again. An hour later, troopers came out to remove it and became physically aggressive with the protesters holding the space. Sergeant John Grinder bulldozed past two of us and grew belligerent. He was openly upset that we were there, peacefully protesting. A couple of his fellow troopers tried to calm him down and walked him into the building tunnel.

While we were technically allowed back on the upper Plaza because of the legalities, they made sure we didn't feel too welcome or comfortable there. Troopers remained outside the door of the capitol from that point on, monitoring us and occasionally bringing out a video camera to record our activities. They also kept barricades up to keep us away from the building. The Plaza belonged to the People, but the capitol remained the private fortress of a governor and his allies in the legislature. The troopers were paid to do their bidding, and they tried to keep us away.

Two days later, on June 25, they raided at 6:30 a.m. I was sitting on a foldable camping chair on the sidewalk. I was trying to keep watch, but I had nodded off to sleep. I woke up surrounded by four troopers staring down at me. It was like a nightmare.

One of the troopers snatched the chair from under me. More troopers rushed out of the tunnel from the capitol building and began taking community donations, signs, chairs, canopies, medications, and other personal items. We were all up at that point, trying to save what we could and make sure everyone was safe.

No matter how many times these raids happened, they never became routine, never something one got used to. They were traumatizing and frightening. My body was in constant fight-or-flight mode. The next few nights I woke up periodically to check if troopers were surrounding me.

I was arrested alone a few days later. A group of us were holding signs and chanting on the upper Plaza, right at the barricades facing the capitol. It was evening, after our General Assembly.

This time I was singled out. They only arrested me.

They had invented another new rule that the upper Plaza—which, to be clear, is outdoors—"closes at 11 p.m." It was around 10 p.m. at that point. I was initially arrested for "inciting a riot" and "criminal trespassing," but the troopers removed the inciting a riot charge after consulting with their superiors.

They brought me to the basement of the capitol to fill out paperwork and then to the jail for booking. I sang the entire time, when they handcuffed and took me away, while they filled out paperwork in the basement, and on the ride in the back of the police car to the jail. I sang and prayed. I knew they wanted me to feel alone, so I did everything I could to connect with the Divine and my ancestors. Hours later I was released.

The more times they arrested us, the less fear there was about it. They took the power out of their ultimate threat by making it routine. The troopers could terrorize us at any time of day or night, and arrest us, but beyond that what could they do? We collectively showed more strength and power by staying, and having the resilience to repair, rebuild, and return after every raid. It was daily resurrection at the doorsteps of state power—power that did not understand that while their authority was dominant, it was not ultimate.

8

Back the Badge?

One thing to note about an occupation: it can get mundane. Things are lively when the troopers swoop in to terrorize and arrest, but the majority of the time we were just a bunch of young people sitting in the sun, trying to bear witness by our presence.

The summer heat only intensified as June wore on. The cement and granite ground beneath us grew hotter. Bottles of water kept in ice coolers became critical; staying hydrated was the only way to sustain ourselves through the brutal Nashville heat in the shadeless Plaza.

A lot of our donations of water and snacks were for mutual aid. Whatever we had was shared with the houseless community around the downtown area, whose members were looking for reprieve from the heat without many options because of the COVID-19 shutdowns. Many folks said that they would usually have gone to the public library a few blocks away for the water fountains and air conditioning, but like most places, it had been closed for months. Anyone who stopped by was free to take any water or snacks that we had and to sit under the canopies. It was a place to rest, which should be a right for us all.

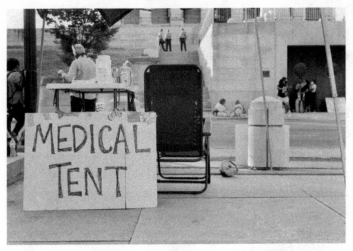

FIGURE 8.1. June 25, 2020. The medical tent was one of the three main canopies set up to support the Plaza occupation as it evolved. Inside were first-aid supplies, hand sanitizer, and face masks. Photo by Ray Di Pietro.

But the troopers continued to raid again and again. Every time they did, they always went for the donated cases of water first. As they descended on the Plaza, they went straight for the food and first-aid canopy, confiscated the stacked cases of water, and threw them in the back of their truck.

Under orders from Governor Bill Lee, it was like they were rewriting Matthew 25: "For I was hungry and you stole our food. I was thirsty and you took our drink. I was a stranger and you threatened to arrest us . . ."

On the sidewalk, some of our folks had written the names of Black lives taken by senseless police killings: Oscar Grant. Sandra Bland. Elijah McClain. Philando Castile. Daniel Hambrick. Atatiana Jefferson. Trayvon Martin. And many others. Artists took the time to carefully write the names as a way to honor the lives lost. It was a beautiful tribute, a way to lift up to passersby why we were still there outside the capitol. The chalked art was washed away naturally by the rain, and in the meantime it brought color and vibrance to the Plaza.

However, at one early morning raid the troopers brought two men with pressure washers. They plundered our supplies as always, took everything down, and then said we had to move so the "sidewalk vandalism" could be cleaned off. It was disrespectful and inhumane. Recalling the last debacle involving troopers and pressure washers, we refused to move.

Some of the young women protesting went over and sat or lay down on the sidewalk as a way to protect the names from being pressure washed away. The troopers gave the order to move, then a few of them tried to physically bully folks out of the way.

Finally the trooper in command said, "It's okay to spray the people too."

And that's exactly what they did. The middle-aged, white gentleman doing the power washing had his co-worker turn on the washer. The fast stream of water shot out, and he started spraying the sidewalk and people, erasing the chalked names. Those on the sidewalk covered their faces from the high-pressure water being shot in their direction as the man made his way up and down the line. Given how hot it was outside, some of the young people made light of the situation by joking about how nice the water felt in the heat. But we all knew how dangerous power washers aimed at people are. The troopers standing around watching and smirking knew it too.

Toward the end of the month, on June 28, a counterprotest was organized to show support for the troopers and police. They

FIGURE 8.2. June 25, 2020. The chalked names of victims of police violence and messages lifting up the demand for racial justice adorn the bronze doors of the Tennessee State Capitol entrance. This act of public witness eventually became a felony offense and those chalking were arrested. Photo by Ray Di Pietro.

called it "Back the Badge," and they planned to hold it right there in the Plaza.

This would increase our threat level significantly. Many of our folks were anxious about what it could mean for our occupation and our safety. We would now be facing threats on two fronts: On one side, the state troopers who had been waging war on us for nearly a month and who we knew would not intervene on our behalf if we were threatened. On the other side, potentially violent counterprotesters with disdain for our cause. These people felt like their way of life was under attack and believed the police kept security and social order. A few of them had been by the Plaza, scoping the area out. A few openly carried firearms. One man frequently took walks by us in the afternoons, with his "God Bless the Police" sign. He always smoked a cigar. This was the group that we would be dealing with.

Our safety team, coordinated by Terry, started preparing extra precautions and ways to keep our space safe and secure while still accessible to the public. There were discussions on how to de-escalate tense situations, ways to keep our folks in a certain area of the Plaza, and a suggestion for a honk-a-thon as a way to drown out counterprotesters in a manner that was safe and allowed social distancing.

A few days before the Back the Badge rally, I went across the street to the barricades to speak with Tennessee Highway Patrol captain Mark Proctor. I shared our concerns for safety and our commitment to nonviolence. He rolled his eyes. I then asked if they were taking any precautions in regard to the counterprotests. He just said they were putting barricades up to divide the groups. Before I could ask any other questions, he said, "That's all I can tell you, Justin," and abruptly walked away.

Rather than reassurance, I left our conversation with confirmation that he had no interest in our group's safety or well-being. We were the only ones who were going to keep us safe. But if there was to be violence, once again, it would not be on our behalf. We continued to meet and plan additional safety measures.

The day of the Back the Badge rally, troopers dragged a few bike racks to divide the middle of the Plaza. Our safety team wore neon-green shirts to stand out and act as a buffer for those staying at the canopies to hold the space. The only tools they had were vigilance and walkie-talkies. All of us were anxious, on edge, and alert.

We remained on the side of the Plaza closest to the capitol; the counterprotesters set up on the opposite side, along Union

Street. They were able to set up canopies for shade and stack cases of water to distribute without any issue. From our vantage point I could see a few large American flags with blue lines through the center and a gaggle of older white men in t-shirts gearing up for their event. The bike racks in the middle of the Plaza were not connected, and the gaps in between made it easy for folks to walk back and forth between sides. The troopers kept their distance back on the capitol steps.

More people continued to arrive as reinforcements to our Ida B. Wells side of the Plaza. We had about two hundred folks blowing bubbles, lining the sidewalk, making colorful art, driving around the Plaza in their cars honking horns, passing out flowers, and playing music as we sought to maintain an upbeat and positive atmosphere to keep tensions low.

The Back the Badge group did not grow any larger than a few dozen people, despite their Facebook group saying hundreds would show up. They were vastly outnumbered. Mostly men, none young, and all white. They began their rally with a few speakers. As they did, the car caravan encircling the perimeter with Black Lives Matter signs blasted car horns to drown them out.

A group of us walked closer to their side to get a better perspective of what was happening and to see what type of rhetoric was being shared. We could make out their signs and shirts, which had messages like "Don't tread on me," "We love our police," "Respect authority," and "Trump 2020." There were also a couple of men with Confederate flags. A lot of conflicting messages.

A few of our folks tried to make conversation and to explain our concerns about police brutality against Black bodies, but that didn't go well. Some of the Back the Badge guys egged

FIGURE 8.3. June 28, 2020. Plaza protesters stand off against "Back the Badge" counterprotesters. The man in the bucket hat and "Don't Tread on Me" flag repeatedly chanted "Back the Badge! Back the Badge!" as the Plaza protesters, linked arm to arm, rhythmically responded with a loud "No!" Photo by Ray Di Pietro.

each other on to get in our faces. One of the counterprotesters eventually walked up to our group and started waving his yellow "Don't tread on me" flag, repeatedly yelling "Back the Badge! Back the Badge! Back the Badge!" He was older, and his only shade was a fishing hat. In the blazing heat, his shouts quickly lost force. Every time he shouted "Back the Badge," our group responded in unison with a collective "No!"

"Back the badge!"

"No!"

"Back the badge!"

"No!"

This back-and-forth went on for a while. We were locked arm in arm, many holding white carnations, and someone had brought over a small drum. More folks from our side came over and held the line until the counterprotesters fizzled out.

After returning to the other side of the Plaza, a large number of us crossed over to the capitol steps. The day was not just about drowning out the hate of counterprotesters, but also about refocusing on our demands for racial justice, reorienting the power of decision making taking place in the building above us, and reclaiming public space that had long been a site of harm. Aside from raids by his henchmen, we still hadn't heard a word from Governor Lee.

We walked up and sat on the cement wall on the perimeter dividing the capitol from the upper Plaza. The troopers on duty quickly rushed forward to tell us to move, and more troopers rushed out of the building. They started to give commands, saying that it was an "unauthorized area, not open to the public" and that we risked arrest if we did not move or if we stepped over the line. These rules continued to be arbitrarily determined. The Plaza belonged to the People and so did the capitol steps. This space was open, but those of us who had been there protesting knew that what was considered open or closed was determined hour by hour.

More people joined us on the barrier, and soon there were about eighty of us lined up with many more standing behind us on the grass. A few of the stragglers from the Back the Badge group came over to spectate and heckle. One lady openly carried her handgun and yelled at some of the Black teenage girls speaking on the megaphone about police violence. We remained on the barrier as troopers lined up in front of us.

One trooper came to me and said, "You either move or be arrested."

I talked with those around me, stood up, and prepared to step down. They could never cite the rules they were making up. Just like in the prior day's struggle simply to walk on the upper Plaza, we posed no safety threat. We had a right to be on public space. If we were being threatened with arrest for merely sitting on the wall, then we might as well step down onto the sidewalk closer to the capitol. After sharing our intentions with those down the line, everyone stood up facing the troopers.

I looked at the young lady next to me and said, "I'm going to step down now." I closed my eyes in prayer and took a step onto the sidewalk. As soon as I did, I was grabbed by a handful of troopers and handcuffed.

"You're under arrest," one of them commanded.

Others standing on the barrier then stepped down as well. Every single person stepping down was arrested, dozens at a time. We were brought around to the back of the building into the capitol basement so troopers could fill out the arrest paperwork.

Some of those protesting did not resist, but used the dead-weight tactic. They let their bodies go limp. The troopers responded by angrily and aggressively lifting them up. Some were almost dropped or carelessly flung and dangled by their arms and legs. The troopers were visibly upset and did not shy away from excessive force. Miss Ruth, one of the older members of the Plaza, had a trooper put his hand in her mouth to force her to raise her head upward, making her stand up. Another young woman who had been helping with the safety team was arrested and had the zip-ties pulled so tight that her hands swelled and turned purple. Once inside the building, other troopers, shocked, struggled to cut them off. The ties left

FIGURE 8.4. June 28, 2020. A day of mass arrests as Plaza protesters line the cement perimeter wall of the Tennessee State Capitol. Almost everyone arrested that afternoon was charged with criminal trespassing on Capitol grounds that were normally open. Photo by Ray Di Pietro.

her with bruises and injuries where the ridge of the plastic had been squeezed into her wrists.

Forty-four of us were arrested and charged with "criminal trespassing." There were so many arrests that the other forty or so people were allowed to remain sitting at the barrier. The troopers did not have the capacity to transport all of us. Those of us arrested were divided up and put into the vans they had waiting to bring us to the jail. We sat for a while as they filled each van.

Most of the young people had never been arrested before. For a few of them it was their first day at the Plaza, and they didn't understand why we were arrested for being on public property in broad daylight. No one I talked to was scared or ashamed, just confused and angry at the process. We watched through the van windows as others were carried over to the back of the capitol where troopers filled out their paperwork inside. We were packed inside the vans like sardines, and it was hot.

After a couple hours or so, when all the vans were completely filled up, they drove us down the street to the Davidson County jail. On the ride over, I kept thinking about how many of us there were who had been arrested. From my experience organizing in Nashville, I figured this had to be one of the largest mass arrests of protesters since the sit-ins of the 1960s. How would they hold us all in the jail?

As we approached the offloading parking garage, troopers and transport personnel radioed each other to get orders about how booking would be handled. The paperwork and booking process for just one person was long and tedious; for forty-four, they would be there all day. We drove in. Each of us was off-boarded from the van one at a time with our hands still zip-tied behind our backs. The trooper cutting off the zip-ties then handed each person a pink piece of paper and said, "You're being cited and released. Your court date is on this paper." It was so strange. They put us through the whole process of being arrested and transported to the jail, then they said we were free to go.

We waited outside the jail garage for a while as others received their citations. A group from the Plaza had walked down for jail support and waited outside as well. Once we had all our folks accounted for, we walked right back to the Plaza to rejoin those remaining outside the capitol holding the space. It was a whirlwind of a day. All of us were tired. Community members had donated a lot of hot food, so we ate dinner, shared experiences, and reconvened for our General Assembly that night.

Early the next morning, troopers swarmed the Plaza and raided again. Five people were arrested. Most were just sitting up talking. After the prior day's activities and mass arrests, no one expected a raid so soon. But the troopers were ready. They arrested folks and cleared the Plaza of community donations, protest signs, cases of water, coolers, chairs, and the houseless population's personal belongings.

Mr. Kingston, an elder member of the Plaza who had passed by and wanted to join the protest, had chronic health issues and was taking the necessary prescribed medications. He diligently came and sat with us almost every day in his baseball cap, holding his protest sign toward the street so all passing traffic could see. All of his medications were taken. It would be a hassle to get refills, and he needed them daily, so we went over to ask where the belongings had been taken, to explain why Mr. Kingston needed his medicine back.

Trooper Edwards replied, "Call him an ambulance, but we can't help you."

He refused to give the names of any supervisors or a number for us to reach them in order to retrieve the medicine. Stealing water and medicine in the middle of the summer heat—there was something especially cruel and inhumane about the activities of the troopers that day, at the behest of Governor Bill Lee. Their intent was never to keep us safe, but even I wouldn't have guessed that it would be so blatantly obvious that they actually meant to harm us.

There are those who might say that it couldn't be all cops or all troopers. That may be true. But there is something each of us witnessed that summer, an overriding impulse: when in that uniform, there is an inevitable gang-like mentality. We experienced their fraternal code of toxic masculinity and blind obedience to orders that made these men, who others might find decent, to act in ways that were callous, barbarous, and ruthless. We all are human beings with faults. However, the power of a badge and a gun should require a raised level of professionalism and decency. Basic humanity. Not just another excuse to brutalize and mistreat others when they think they can get away with it. It was that reality of mistreatment and abuse by law enforcement that brought us out into the streets and onto the Plaza in the first place. Rather than heed our concerns about the crisis of police violence, they responded with more of the same.

In response to the events of June 28 and 29, we released the following statement:

> On Sunday, June 28, 2020, the Tennessee Highway Patrol arrested 38 protesters for "criminal trespassing" while setting foot on the capitol during business hours. Less than 24 hours later, at 6:20 A.M. on Monday, June 29, four protesters and one minor present at the protest site were arrested and charged with "camping on state property," although there were no tents. The troopers also raided the Plaza and seized canopies providing shade, food, and essential supplies. During the arrests on Sunday, many protesters were pulled off the wall by troopers, obtained injuries and wounds, and were kept outside in the heat for hours with little water and no food or shade. People of all ages were arrested, and excessive force was used on the elderly as well. These were recorded on video by numerous witnesses. Protesters have remained peaceful throughout the duration of the protest. These latest arrests are efforts by the Governor and the THP to discourage and dismiss these protests. Over the last 16 days, THP has continually escalated the situation through

physical violence and the arbitrary imposition of laws that are changed daily. The latest arrests occurring on Monday are in direct response to the progress made and retaliation to the solidarity shown on Sunday. We know that we are making progress, not only because of the tremendous support from the Nashville community, but because we are reaching individual troopers as well. After weeks-long conversation with our protesters, one state trooper has made the decision to no longer work security at the Plaza, and refuses to be used as Governor Lee's personal intimidation force any longer to keep the people from their Plaza. We will continue to occupy the Plaza and exercise our First Amendment right to protest until Governor Bill Lee meets with organizers to have a conversation about our concerns or until the bust of Confederate General and Ku Klux Klan leader Nathan Bedford Forrest is removed from the Capitol building.

Early in the morning a few days later, before the sun had yet come up, a few troopers began circling the Plaza flashing their lights and putting sirens on. They were riding by to harass those of us who had held the space all night. The troopers did not get out of their vehicles or make any other contact. They just rode by blaring sirens and flashing the lights on their cars. When they got to the end of the street, they turned them off, circled the block, and did it again. It was clear that they wanted to make sure we didn't doze off or feel relaxed.

This is how we ended the month of June. Psychological warfare and intimidation. Bullying.

It remains deeply disturbing that grown men acted this way toward a group of mainly young people—young people they were supposedly hired to protect. At what point did they lose sight of our humanity, of their own? When did they stop seeing us as someone else's children, as human beings who wanted better for our future, as people in a public space that belongs to all of us?

This was terror, plain and simple. It might have felt like a game to them, but it was cruel.

9

"It Was Like We Were Being Hunted"

On July 1, we got an unexpected announcement. Governor Bill Lee released a press statement saying that the Capitol Commission—the state panel with the authority to begin the removal process for the Ku Klux Klan monument in Tennessee's capitol—was scheduled to meet and take up the issue. We were shocked. This was one of our key demands at the Plaza, as our statement had articulated.

Throughout our time holding the space, Governor Lee would not meet with us. Despite repeated requests, he refused. He declined even to meet with elected members of the Black Caucus. He and his office acted like they were ignoring our concerns every time our presence in the Plaza was brought up at his weekly press conferences.

This announcement was also an abrupt shift from the previous year and from Lee's statements prior to assuming office—when he made his position against removal of the monument very clear.

In January 2019, he told reporters, "I've said oftentimes I think the removal of monuments is not the best approach to resolving the challenges that are presented with that conversation. . . . Wiping out history wipes out, also, the history that we're not proud of."

Lee then went on to make correlations between revisionist narratives, or attempts to "whitewash history" as he put it. As governor-elect he stated, "The Ku Klux Klan is a part of our history that we're not proud of in Tennessee, and we need to be reminded of that and make certain that we don't forget it. So I wouldn't advocate to remove that."

It was a position he had long held. It was not until that summer, as we camped outside and kept the pressure for racial justice on him, that his public comments and position began to shift. This was a step forward. It felt like a small victory for the movement.

The Capitol Commission was set to meet the following week. We started to wonder if troopers would be ordered to try and preemptively clear out the Plaza before the vote as a precaution. Once again, anxiety walked among the folks holding the space. But we remained.

Removing the monument to Nathan Bedford Forrest—a slaver, Confederate, and KKK grand wizard—from the state capitol was the lowest-hanging fruit. Some asked why we even chose to include it among our demands alongside racial justice policy and demilitarizing the police. But the connection between this symbol of white supremacist terror and the harm perpetrated against Black people was too blatant to ignore. This monument was placed in the capitol in 1978 as a message of resistance to the Civil Rights Movement a decade after Dr. Martin Luther King Jr.'s assassination in Tennessee. The same week it was put up, a cross was burned outside the Nashville NAACP. The monument was a hostile message to Black Tennesseans, a standing notice that we were not welcome in the People's House. It honored a man who terrorized, enslaved, and massacred our forebears.

More importantly, it was a litmus test. If we could not remove such a blatant symbol and icon of racism, then how would we succeed in removing the more subtle and sophisticated policies of racism that we were challenging. Rev. Sonnye Dixon, a retired Methodist pastor and former president of the Nashville NAACP, came to the Plaza and addressed this very issue when he spoke to us at our General Assembly that week. He shared the story of being a child and being asked by an elder woman for a piece of candy. She said, "I know that if you won't give me something that insignificant, then when we ask you for something that's really important, you won't give it to me." Removal of this Ku Klux Klan monument was like that piece of candy—seemingly trivial, but an important precedent for the substantive matters ahead.

The vote was scheduled for July 9, 2020. In the meantime, we organized and encouraged community members to contact the twelve Capitol Commission members. I left Tennessee for the July Fourth holiday weekend—to demonstrate for a couple of days in Washington, DC—but planned to be back in time for the commission meeting. It was my first time being physically away from the Plaza protests for a substantial period, but we were a "leader-ful movement" and had many good folks holding things down. I kept in touch with what was going on through calls and texts.

July Fourth was an explosive day on the Plaza. A march led by the Teens for Equality group converged at the capitol. It started as a celebration in the Plaza with music, saxophones, and dancing as resistance to a holiday celebrating counterfeit freedom: Freedom for a small portion of America. Not for many of our ancestors. Not for us.

The Department of Safety, in anticipation of the day's march, had arbitrarily "closed" the upper Plaza for the weekend. The troopers had brought their metal bike racks back out and placed them in front of the stairs.

Some of the Plaza organizers helping to lead the day's actions made the decision not to allow people to again be pushed away from public space for no legitimate reason. They climbed the hill to the upper Plaza. Hundreds of troopers descended from the capitol. It was one of their largest shows of force. But those holding down the Plaza, mostly young people and almost all women, didn't back down. In response, the troopers didn't hold back. When they ordered people to leave, the protesters stood firm. Organizers at the Plaza showed immense courage and stepped up to lead those days' actions.

The protesters grouped together. Some laid down their bodies to protect one another on the upper Plaza. The troopers surrounded them. Then, these large men in uniform groped at them, dragged folks down the concrete steps, pushed some people off the large barrier wall, and did not spare demonstrations of aggression. An eleven-year-old girl who was on the grass watching with her family was told to jump off the large concrete wall or face arrest. A young man was pulled down by his hair. These were the actions of troopers charged with protecting and serving Tennesseans.

It was another traumatic day. The Fourth of July.

Those who were arrested stayed in jail well into the afternoon of July 5. The troopers reported thirty-three people were

FIGURE 9.1. July 4, 2020. Terry leads chants as protesters enter the upper Plaza during July Fourth protests at the capitol. The state troopers later declared the area closed by order of the Tennessee Department of Safety and Homeland Security commissioner Jeff Long. Photo by Ray Di Pietro.

arrested, almost all for "criminal trespassing" on a public space. While all this was happening, fireworks went off in the distance on the river, visible from Capitol Hill.

I returned on July 6 to find a strong group that was still processing the trauma of what had happened. The stories and images were haunting. Talking to friends, seeing bruises, and hearing the amount of violence leveraged against protesters was heavy. Even in the jail, they suffered. Some people were put into isolation; while trapped in there, pepper spray was deployed in the adjacent cell, making it difficult to breathe. Another new friend from the Plaza, a science fiction author and graduate student, was literally dragged by her hands and feet by troopers. They showed me the video. It was horrific.

Yet, despite all this, people remained in the Plaza, holding the space, anxiously awaiting the Capitol Commission vote set to happen just a few days later. I considered whether this brutality was a sign that they would vote against removing the monument. Maybe they were trying to force us out as a precaution. Would their violence escalate?

It did.

On July 7, 2020, many of us were taken in a night of mass arrests. We had marched across the street and lined the cement barrier wall with our hands up. We stood chanting and facing down the battalion of state troopers deployed outside the capitol building. They ordered us to step down and move back. When we did not, twelve of us were arrested. Those arrested included two freelance photojournalists, Alex Kent and David Piñeros, who had identified themselves and clearly had cameras. Alex had even asked permission to take photos. None of that mattered. One by one, we were taken to the back of the capitol to be placed in the arrest vans. I sang "This Little Light of Mine" as troopers pushed me to walk faster. In the back of the capitol, they had a setup where they had us take photos with our arresting officers for their records.

They loaded us in vans. They drove us to the mobile booking unit by the stadium. Then they drove us to the Davidson County jail.

In jail, we went through another booking process and an hour later we were able to use the phones. I tried to call our legal observer, Niti Sharan, who had been with us since the first week of the protests. She was a lawyer in Florida who had recently returned home to Tennessee and was documenting rights violations, helping us with bail support, and getting in

FIGURE 9.2. July 7, 2020. Justin sings "This Little Light of Mine" after being arrested. State troopers started taking photos with arresting officers and protesters' arrest information to keep track of the hundreds of arrests. Photo courtesy of Tennessee Department of Safety and Homeland Security.

touch with other attorneys who were members of the Tennessee Bar Association for assistance.

I kept calling, but could not get an answer. The phone went straight to voicemail. This was unusual; Niti and others volunteering to coordinate legal support were usually really good about answering calls from inside the jail. I went to the phones again. Tried to call. Straight to voicemail. A couple of other people who were making calls then started to get word that there had been another raid at the Plaza. That's all they knew.

I went back to sit down on the male side of the holding room. The officers kept chastising us for trying to talk back and forth to see if anyone had any updates. How many people were arrested? Who? We had no idea.

I sat down, not knowing who to call. Hours passed. It was around two in the morning. Still no updates. Then I saw Niti and a few other women from the Plaza being brought into the jail. I was half asleep, and I was not expecting to see support team on the inside being booked. Niti's long black hair, which was usually up in a bun, flowed down. They released her hands from the handcuffs.

"Niti!" I said. "What's going on? What happened?"

"They arrested everyone," she said.

Apparently, after arresting the original twelve of us, troopers went down and arrested every single person left in the Plaza. Forty-seven more people were arrested. Protesters. Houseless community. Those just stopping by to observe. It did not matter. Troopers trapped people in the Plaza from all sides and swarmed in from various entrances.

I still didn't quite understand the extent of what was going on. Niti said she was arrested standing in the street, not even by the canopies, but was charged with "illegal camping." All of our houseless friends and community members, some of whom were just in the vicinity of the Plaza, were picked up and arrested as well. The Plaza was totally cleared. More folks started to trickle into the jail. We were in shock.

"It was like we were being hunted," said Niti.

During these escalating night raids, the troopers would rush out unannounced from all sides in the dark of night. There was no warning. No, "You're under arrest." A group of troopers would just swarm around and arrest people one by one. The troopers utilized the tunnels underneath us (connecting buildings on Capitol Hill) to position themselves to rush out for raids. They moved beneath us. And with an elaborate camera system around the capitol and new cameras placed around the Plaza—the extent of which we only learned about much later—they were watching us at all times. It was like a horror movie.

As more people were processed and brought in from the mass arrests, the holding area soon filled up and got crowded. The guards in the jail grew more irritable as their workload drastically increased.

"Damn! Who the hell are all these people," one of them yelled across the room.

We started to have a reunion in the jail as Plaza folks were brought in. They shared more stories about what had happened, property being taken, and the aggressiveness of the troopers. Everyone was exhausted. The phones were periodically cut off. When they turned the phones back on, we made calls out to relatives and community members who had not been at the protest to make arrangements for bail for those who would need it. We could only call the numbers we had memorized or the few we had written down, since the majority of our personal items had been taken at booking, including our phones. Bail amounts fluctuated. Some people would be released on pretrial without need for bail. My bail that night was set at $1,000.

We sat down in our assigned sections, making hand gestures to communicate updates on people's release statuses. The guard in the middle kept chastising us and said we could not talk to each other or we would be put into isolation cells. One of the guards, Johnson, grew increasingly belligerent and made derogatory remarks to some of the women being booked. The influx of arrestees and the lateness of the night greatly increased tensions.

I started to sing, "Wait, in the Plaza . . . Wait, in the Plaza, children . . . Wait . . ." and others quickly joined in. We sang and chanted for a little, until the guards grew angry and told us to be quiet. They said it could be interpreted as "starting a riot."

I started to sing again. Johnson had enough.

"I think it's time he went upstairs," he told the other guards. "His bond hadn't been processed. Go change him."

I had no idea what this meant. I had never been "upstairs." My bond had already been paid, but the paperwork hadn't been processed yet with the influx of people. As another guard walked over to me, Niti jumped up.

"Here," she said. "Let me pay his bond on my credit card. I'll pay his bond." I think she saw the uncertainty in my face. None of us had been taken upstairs at that point—and being separated was never a safe option.

"Nope," the guard said. He walked me to a room behind the holding area. He was a white man with a black baseball cap and an American flag tattoo. I had no idea what this process was.

"What's back here?" I asked.

"You have to change," he said. "What's your sizes? Tell them."

After getting my new clothes to change into from the counter, we walked to a stall at the end of the hall. He handed me an orange jumpsuit, white boxer shorts, and orange laceless shoes to change into.

"Change in here?" I asked.

"Yup," he said, and then walked into the stall with me. We stood there silently. "What are you waiting for?" he said, irritated.

"For you to step out so I can change," I replied. I had never had to change my clothes any other time I was arrested. It was humiliating having to strip and change in front of another man who was glaring at me. I kept my clothes on. "I don't feel comfortable," I told him.

"Well, we can force you to change. So you better hurry up." I was horrified.

Then he said, "I have to search you for contraband too."

What in the world was happening? The violation I felt in that moment was scarring. I thought of slave auctions and Black bodies being inspected by those who saw them as property. It was dehumanizing. As he threatened to get more guards to force me to cooperate, I started to recite Psalm 23 aloud as I changed out of my clothes and was searched.

"The Lord is my Shepherd, I shall not want," I began. I just wanted to be outside of my body in that experience. I continued to recite the Psalm. "He makes me lie down in green pastures, he leads me beside the still waters, he restores my soul."

"Face me and hurry up," he ordered.

"He leads me in the right paths, for His name's sake. Even though I walk through the Valley of the Shadow of Death, I will fear no evil for You are with me . . ."

When it was done, the man walked me out to the isolation cell by the holding area to wait before being brought upstairs. Another guard took my clothes and gave me a blanket, a bag with hygiene supplies, and a small laminated card with my picture, name, and a number. For race, they had put "WHITE."

I passed Niti and others as I walked by in my orange jumpsuit. They made hand signals to give me encouragement. As I waited in the isolation cell, I could see them through the glass window. One young woman wrote notes on the tiny papers available in the holding area with messages of support and humor. She held them up when the guards weren't looking. I could barely read them, but they made me feel less alone. When one guard finally did see her, she was placed into an isolation cell as well.

A couple of hours passed. It was morning. I thought I was just going to stay in that room, and that was okay with me. But then two more guards came.

"Jones," one said sternly. "Time to go upstairs."

They walked me to the back down a long hallway to elevators.

"I heard you like to pray," one of the guards escorting me said as we walked. "Well, didn't you see in the Bible where it says 'obey authority'?" he said, smirking.

I kept silent as we got on the elevator.

"I tend to ascribe more to the story in Exodus and the Bible's message of releasing captives," I finally replied as we rode up. The guards chuckled.

We walked through two more security doors, and they brought me up another set of stairs to a cell. The door had no handle; it was controlled by a switch elsewhere. It opened for me to walk in. Another man was sleeping inside. I walked in and the door closed shut with a metal clack that sounded permanent. My heart dropped. I climbed to the top bunk, as the man was sound asleep on the bottom. The room was completely white. No way to use phones or communicate with others. Just waiting. I sat with my legs crossed, closed my eyes, and continued to pray.

The hours passed, and the man below me woke up. He was happy to have someone to talk to. He had been there a few days without a cellmate. He explained what it meant to be upstairs, and not to have access to phones until later. We just sat in that room talking, surrounded by nothing but white walls and concrete. Coincidentally, we had the same name. He had seen some of the coverage of our protests on the news a couple weeks prior.

"When I get out, I'm gonna stop by there. At the capitol, right?" he said.

I was grateful for the understanding and conversation he offered to help ease my worries.

Around noon, a guard came by to let me know my bond was processed and I would be released. They gave me paperwork to fill out. I waited a few more hours.

I was the only one brought upstairs that night. It was the one time I second-guessed my presence in the Plaza. But as I walked out of the jail, I was greeted by friends outside who cheered and rushed to give me hugs. I was out. This community was why I continued. We returned to join those who had set the Plaza back up, and resumed the occupation. We weren't leaving.

Night Terror

The Capitol Commission vote was the very next day, July 9, 2020; we didn't have much time to slow down. We finalized plans for gathering outside the commission meeting. We knew that the vote could go either way, and we wanted to make a large show of support for removal of the Forrest bust. We needed to make the message clear that it was time for that monument—and the racist policies it represented—to be brought down.

There was so much energy that day, a day we had been waiting for. I had been at the last Capitol Commission meeting about removing the monument in September 2017, when the commission voted to block then governor Bill Haslam's request for it to be removed amid public pressure. It was disappointing. Not many people had been in attendance, and the commission had overwhelmingly voted against removal. This time was different. Public pressure had swelled and two hundred or more of us were gathered outside between the capitol and the Tennessee Tower, where the vote was to be held. We just hoped the vote result would be different as well.

A large group of us walked over to the Tennessee Tower to try to observe the commission meeting and see if there would

FIGURE 10.1. July 22, 2020. Dragon. A list of the Plaza's demands can be partially seen in the background. Photo by Ray Di Pietro.

be any opportunity for public comment. Others stayed on the Plaza making art, playing music, and holding signs for cars driving by. There was so much excitement. Everyone was on edge.

As soon as we entered the Tennessee Tower, we were stopped at the security gate. The security guard was from a private company and said he didn't know the protocol for public access. He called a trooper to find out. The trooper came over and informed us that members of the public would not be allowed inside the commission meeting because of COVID-19 restrictions.

"What about the public comment period?" someone asked.

"You got to talk to the commission staff about that."

We waited there in the lobby as more of our folks came in and filled the space, overflowing into the courtyard outside. As it got closer to meeting time, staff started to arrive from the Office of the State Architect, who was coordinating the meeting.

A woman informed us that no other public comments would be accepted because the deadline had passed, though none of us had known the deadline date or process for getting on the public comment list to begin with. More attendees started to arrive, including State Representative Mike Sparks of Murfreesboro. He was publicly against removal. As he walked through our ranks in the lobby to enter the meeting, Justin Kanew, an independent journalist with the *Tennessee Holler* media site, stopped him for an interview.

"Was the Civil War fought over slavery?" he asked State Representative Sparks.

"I haven't really studied it," Sparks replied.

People in the crowd started to ask follow-up questions about how Sparks had berated others for not knowing history in previous years and why he continued to be a passionate defender of Nathan Bedford Forrest's legacy in the legislature.

"We all need to study our history," Sparks deflected. "You know there's different contexts, different interpretations." This was the same representative who had faced backlash from the Black Caucus in 2017 for sneaking a resolution honoring Nathan Bedford Forrest's story of redemption through the House's routine consent calendar.

Others began to arrive, including commission members and state lawmakers like State Representative G. A. Hardaway and State Senator Brenda Gilmore, who were both in support of removal. Tennessee Secretary of State Tre Hargett walked right by us and refused to acknowledge anyone or answer questions as people asked for clarification on his 2017 vote to keep the Ku Klux Klan monument up.

More troopers were stationed outside in the hallways as well, keeping an eye on us and making sure we stayed behind the security gate. We did. But we chanted. Since we weren't allowed in the meeting, we wanted our voices and support for removal of the monument to be heard. Chants of "Whose House? Our House!" echoed off the walls. Soon some staff members came out to the lobby asking us to settle down. They could hear us loudly in the room where the commission was meeting and said it was disrupting business. The governor began to speak to the commission members. He had entered through another entrance to avoid the likes of us. Other lawmakers spoke as well. We listened through the video livestream on our phones. A couple of people held phones to a megaphone so everyone could hear the discussion inside the meeting.

State Senator Joey Hensley got up to make clear his position for keeping the monument up.

"Three thousand Blacks were at his funeral," he said. "Forrest was in the Ku Klux Klan, but he was not a grand wizard."

These were the types of arguments being made by Forrest apologists at that meeting. None were grounded in facts.

I sat next to a protester who had driven from Memphis for the day's events. We watched the livestream intently on a small phone screen, reacting to the offhand comments defending Forrest and hoping that the commission would finally do the right thing. People continued to fill up the lobby. Some anxiously walked in and back outside as we waited for the vote. More people overflowed outside the building and sat on the steps in front of the Tennessee Tower.

The meeting went on for hours.

A lawyer for the Sons of Confederate Veterans group was allowed to speak and offer public comment. The amount of mental gymnastics that went into trying to redeem the legacy of a man who massacred and terrorized Black people was

FIGURE 10.2. July 9, 2020. Justin, Niti (far right), and other protesters gather at the base of the pedestal where Edward Carmack's statue once stood to celebrate the Capitol Commission's overwhelming vote to initiate the process to remove the bust of KKK grand wizard Nathan Bedford Forrest from the Tennessee capitol. Photo by Ray Di Pietro.

astonishing. I kept thinking to myself, imagine if they showed this much care and concern for the protection of actual human beings' lives—the very issues we were lifting up in the Plaza around police brutality.

At last, after lengthy discussion and comments among its members, the commission got to the roll-call vote. All of us grew silent. One person held up her hands in the front, using her fingers to keep track as commission members' names were called one by one with a response of "Aye" or "Nay" for removal.

In the final vote, nine members voted for removal. State Senator Jack Johnson and State Representative Matthew Hill were the only two to vote against it.

Those of us crowded in the lobby erupted into cheers. People started hugging those around them and jumping for joy. The Capitol Commission had actually done the right thing. The process would now proceed to the Tennessee Historical Commission to take up the waiver request. Though we knew there were still additional processes and votes, we vigorously celebrated getting past this initial hurdle.

Rev. Venita got on the megaphone and began to wail out, "Wait, in the Plaza . . . Wait, in the Plaza, children . . ." Everyone joined in. Some people brought drums and the beat was like thunder in the hallway.

"I believe that we will win! I believe that we will win!" we all chanted. Clapping and jumping. Yelling aloud in joy. My voice grew hoarse. After all our spirits, bodies, and minds had endured the past few weeks in the Plaza, the celebration was liberating.

It continued at the Plaza as we returned. Others joined us. People crossed the street to chant and dance on the upper Plaza, in front of the capitol where the bust's days were numbered.

"Ain't no party like a liberation party, because a liberation party don't stop! Say what?" people chanted. They held up signs with messages like "Don't Memorialize the KKK," "Black Lives Are Sacred," and "No KKK in Our Capitol." The celebration continued through the night. All of those who had been holding down the Plaza needed it. It was a release. An exhale.

Some began to question if we should pack up and end the occupation since the vote for removal had been successful. One of our demands had been met. But the overall consensus was to stay. Removal of the monument was just one of our demands. Plus, Forrest would remain in the capitol until the Tennessee Historical Commission voted on the waiver; it was still uncertain

FIGURES 10.3. AND 10.4. July 9, 2020. Protesters celebrate on the Plaza after the Capitol Commission voted to initiate the process to remove the bust of KKK grand wizard Nathan Bedford Forrest from the Tennessee Capitol. This was a demand of the Plaza protest from the beginning. Photos by Ray Di Pietro.

when that vote would actually happen. Considering all these factors, we remained in the Plaza.

The days of celebration were short-lived. Just two days after the Capitol Commission vote, the troopers resumed mass arrests and launched a new strategy of targeting those they deemed to be organizers of the protests.

Earlier in the day, our friend Blaylock—a member of the houseless community who joined us and volunteered at the food tent serving folks—had been rushed by troopers for standing at the barricades speaking on the megaphone. A trooper snatched the megaphone, saying it was "disorderly conduct," and others rushed forward to grab him. In the rush, Blaylock fell down the concrete steps and broke his jaw. Even while he was in the emergency room, the troopers went to the magistrate to get a warrant for his arrest. After hearing the facts about what had happened, the warrant was repeatedly denied.

That night, July 11, 2020, during a direct-action march around the capitol, we stopped at the back barricades chanting, "Wake up, wake up! We want freedom, freedom! All these racist state troopers, we don't need 'em, need 'em!" A friend who had joined the Plaza protests the previous week led us in another new chant: "Blaylock didn't do nothing, so we gon' do something!"

State Senator Jeff Yarbro had spoken to our General Assembly that evening. He remained with us, standing in the background with Niti, observing as we marched and chanted at the back barricades. We stood at the metal bike racks linked together in the back of the capitol as a barrier. We raised our voices but did not cross the barrier. No matter. Troopers ran out without any warning toward those of us gathered. They started grabbing people to arrest. People ran away not knowing what was happening. Even Senator Yarbro was surprised and tried to get the troopers to stop.

"Come on, guys!" he exclaimed. None of this mattered to them. The troopers were after specific people this time, and they came straight for them.

When armed men run at you like they are about to tackle you on a football field, the only logical response is to run. I ran. No commands to stop or arrest orders were given. They just came at us with the intensity of a hunt. I nearly tumbled down the hill. Everyone was scattered. Seven people were arrested.

Some of those not arrested returned to the Plaza, while the rest of us regrouped in the parking lot outside the jail for bail and legal support. We stopped by the night magistrate's office and looked online to check the status of those arrested. It was another long night. I sat in the car with Niti and Mohamed, waiting. Finally, Niti got a call from inside. Another main organizer of the logistics who kept the Plaza going had been one of those targeted for arrest. She had an update we needed to hear. As she was being transported, she overheard the trooper's radio saying that they were gearing up to make another raid on the Plaza that night. It was after midnight. It could happen at any time. Niti and Mohamed decided to go back up to the Plaza to check on those there and to give them the heads-up to be on alert for a possible raid. I stayed outside the jail, waiting in the car for those who we hoped would get out soon. I started to doze off, waiting for a phone call from inside. I closed my eyes.

Knock! Knock! Knock!

I was jolted awake. Mohamed was banging on the window.

"What's going on, Mohamed?" I was completely confused and startled. He reached through the window and put his hand on my shoulder.

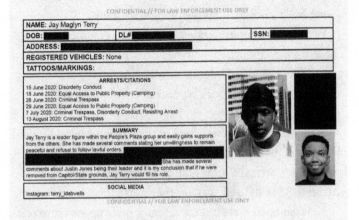

CONFIDENTIAL // FOR LAW ENFORCEMENT USE ONLY

NAME: Jay Maglyn Terry		
DOB: ▮	DL# ▮	SSN: ▮
ADDRESS: ▮		
REGISTERED VEHICLES: None		
TATTOOS/MARKINGS:		

ARRESTS/CITATIONS
15 June 2020: Disorderly Conduct
18 June 2020: Equal Access to Public Property (Camping)
28 June 2020: Criminal Trespass
29 June 2020: Equal Access to Public Property (Camping)
7 July 2020: Criminal Trespass, Disorderly Conduct, Resisting Arrest
13 August 2020: Criminal Trespass

SUMMARY
Jay Terry is a leader figure within the People's Plaza group and easily gains supports from the others. She has made several comments stating her unwillingness to remain peaceful and refusal to follow lawful orders. ▮ She has made several comments about Justin Jones being their leader and it is my conclusion that if he were removed from Capitol/State grounds, Jay Terry would fill his role.

SOCIAL MEDIA
Instagram: terry_idabwells

CONFIDENTIAL // FOR LAW ENFORCEMENT USE ONLY

FIGURE 10.5. Jay Terry's profile from "People's Plaza TN Significant Personnel (more than 2 arrests)," the Tennessee Highway Patrol's dossier on the People's Plaza protests, obtained through a public records request in January 2021. The dossier includes information on protesters' families, social media, and love lives. Courtesy of Tennessee Department of Safety and Homeland Security.

"They arrested Niti, brother. They raided," he said. Niti and Mohamed had not even been on the Plaza grounds when the arrests were made. They were at Mohamed's car on Sixth Avenue. Prior to the raid, a trooper came out to them, saying he could not let Niti leave. Then they made arrests and charged her with "illegal camping" once again. They had targeted all those deemed to be leaders in the Plaza. It was blatant.

Much later, through a public records request, we saw just how coordinated the troopers' surveillance and analysis of the Plaza had been. We received a scanned, redacted packet with profiles of some of the core occupants of the Plaza, including pictures taken from social media, THP's assessments of where each fell in our leadership—and what would happen if they were to be "removed." It is a chilling document.

With more people arrested, those who remained gathered outside for jail support. All who had been arrested were released by morning, exhausted but not surrendering to the terror being leveraged by the governor's troopers.

It was July 12, 2020. We returned to the Plaza for what marked one month there. A full month of holding the space down despite raids, arrests, and theft of property by troopers. We remained. That in itself was another cause for celebration.

New canopies were put up. A tent was set up for art to celebrate the occasion. Plaza artists screen printed original designs commemorating the day onto t-shirts. One had an image of broken chains with the words "Breaking the chains at Ida B. Wells Plaza" printed above. That's exactly what we were fighting to do. Just hours after being arrested, our folks were right back in the Plaza. Shining light. Breaking chains.

It was another day of music and community, lifting up our struggles and joys together. More cars stopped by with people who had heard what was going on and brought donations of food and supplies to sustain our sit-in.

"Don't let up. I just wish I could do more," one woman said while we unloaded her trunk of grocery donations. Her little daughter sat in the back smiling. She was four.

"Show them what you learned," her mom said.

The little girl smiled shyly. She raised her fist in her booster seat and softly said, "Power to the people."

These were the experiences and stories that collectively were breaking the chains. The city knew what was happening in the Plaza. People of all ages and races, and from all regions in the

FIGURE 10.6. July 12, 2020. Artists screen print People's Plaza designs onto t-shirts to mark one month of the Plaza occupation. Photo by Ray Di Pietro.

state came by to show support, even if it was just to drop off more supplies. We had a Facebook support group of ladies who communicated about ongoing needs at the Plaza, like one who came from Bedford County, and another constant supporter all the way from hours away in rural East Tennessee. I called them our "movement grandmothers"; they were guardians and just as much a part of the Plaza as those who were physically there every day. We sustained that space together and everyone had a role that made it possible.

Later that night we had a General Assembly meeting and, as we did every night, took a vote on whether to stay another day. People voted enthusiastically to stay.

Afterward, people marched across the street for a direct-action rally at the barricades. It was still early; the troopers' directive had made clear that the space was not "closed" until

11 p.m. Others went first. I stayed behind talking to a few folks, then walked up to join the group as people started to chant at the barricades. Before I could reach the top, just as I was walking up the last few steps, troopers rushed into the upper Plaza. I stepped backward as people ran away, but I was stopped at the bottom steps by troopers who had popped out of the tunnel between staircases to trap us. I was surrounded by the dozens of troopers who had rushed down and more who joined them as reinforcements.

They handcuffed me and said they had a warrant for my arrest. I was the only one arrested. One of the troopers from the night before falsely accused me of assaulting him with a megaphone when we all ran away. The truth we all knew was that this was just more of their targeting tactics, trying to isolate those they had deemed to be organizers of the protests. I waited in jail and was released around 3 a.m. after posting bond.

Most of the people at the Plaza had moved to the parking lot outside the jail because of fears of another raid that night. Some people felt it was time to pack up and leave the Plaza; we all recognized the escalation of the troopers, and we knew they would likely arrest any of us who returned. If they raided and arrested all of us, the Plaza would be empty anyway. Many folks recommended we leave and return later in the morning, when it was daylight.

I shared my intention to go right back. If we backed down, the troopers' intimidation tactics would have been successful. I invited those willing to join and a few of us returned to sit outside on the Plaza, on the sidewalk, holding signs through the rest of the night. My sign read "Jail Won't Break Us."

We sat there prepared to be arrested. I was grateful for the courage of those who came back and stayed there facing off with the troopers. We sat with our eyes toward the capitol. The troopers came out in a line on the railing to count how many of us were there. They kept coming out, making gestures and maneuvers indicating arrests to follow. A group of them literally came out to stand on the upper Plaza looking down at us, pointing like they were going to make arrests. They even put on the black rubber gloves that were used when they raided and arrested folks. Everything they did signaled arrests to come. We remained. If they arrested us, that's what would happen.

One young woman, who also worked as a licensed therapist, said, "We're too tired, and tired of running." We remained.

The troopers lined the railing and capitol steps. I looked at those around me: Everyone sat still and unbothered. We had all already surrendered to the inevitable. Niti circled in a car, ready to provide jail support. The troopers kept communicating back and forth to each other and making hand gestures. Arrest was imminent.

Then the troopers left and went back inside the capitol.

Was it a trick? Would daylight find us in the Plaza or in jail? We sat there, talking to each other. Someone played an audiobook on a loudspeaker. We remained. And the morning sunlight came. We had made it through the night. We were not broken. And the sit-in continued.

More reinforcements arrived in the morning and throughout the day. We set the canopies back up and resumed serving meals, distributing water, and holding signs outside the capitol.

The ACLU and the governor's office had exchanged letters regarding the People's Plaza on July 2, 6, and 9. The ACLU's July 2 letter demanded an explanation for the raids and property seizures, and the July 9 letter pinpointed the flaw in the governor's legal logic:

> Your letter relies on T.C.A. § 39-14-414 as authority for the seizure of personal property. The use of this statute to seize personal property is the problem. The statute affords absolutely no due process and requires no warrant before a seizure may take place. It simply dictates that seizure of property is authorized. This directly contravenes the Constitution.
>
> The first clause of the Fourth Amendment provides that the "right of the people to be secure in their persons, houses, papers and effects, against unreasonable searches and seizures, shall not be violated." U.S. Const. Amend. IV. This clause protects against two types of intrusions of a person's property: "searches" and "seizures." *United States v. Jacobsen*, 466 U.S. 109, 113 (1984). . . .
>
> A seizure without a warrant is "per se unreasonable. The Government bears the burden of showing that a warrantless search or seizure falls within an exception to the Fourth Amendment's warrant requirement." *United States v. Cervantes*, 703 F.3d 1135, 1141 (9th Cir. 2012). And even if a search or seizure is lawful at its inception, the seizure "can nevertheless violate the Fourth Amendment because its manner of execution unreasonably infringes possessory interests protected by the Fourth Amendment's prohibition on 'unreasonable seizures.'" *Jacobsen*, 466 U.S. at 124-25. . . .
>
> Your July 6 letter indicates that "non-perishable items" removed from the Plaza for violations of the anti-camping statute (Tenn. Code Ann. 39-14-414), but "not required to be maintained as evidence," could be retrieved at the THP headquarters. This is beside the point. Simply providing a

FIGURE 10.7. August 4, 2020. Justin shows local media how easy it is to wipe the chalked names and statements off the bronze doors of the Capitol building using a paper towel and water. State troopers were charging people with felony vandalism for chalking because they claimed it cost over $2,000 to clean. Photo by Ray Di Pietro.

means to retrieve unconstitutionally seized property does not erase the violation of the 4th and 14th Amendments.

Raids let up over the next few days, but we still found ourselves outside the jail a lot more as the targeted arrests continued. The troopers would now only arrest individuals. They obtained arrest warrants for specific people from Tennessee attorney general Herbert Slatery's office. They had also started arresting people for writing the names of Black lives taken by police violence in chalk on the bronze doors of the capitol. The troopers said it was felony vandalism because it cost $2,000 to clean—even though the chalk effortlessly washed off with a bottle of water and a paper towel, as we illustrated for the media. What they labeled and criminalized as vandalism, was in fact another public act of reclamation. Writing the names of victims of state violence on the state house doors can be described as nothing less.

These types of arrests became more common. It was another form of terror that had us all on guard and wondering who they would try to pick off next.

July 17, 2020, found us again waiting outside the jail. A friend had been arrested. I had just walked out of the night magistrate's office where we were trying to get information on the false charges against our friend. I was sitting outside the jail with another Plaza organizer, checking updates on my phone. I will never forget that moment because it was there and then that we learned that John Lewis had passed away. C. T. Vivian, another civil rights giant, had passed earlier that same day. Both of these legends had begun their involvement right where we were, in Nashville, with the sit-ins and Freedom Rides.

When I was interning in DC in 2016, I popped into Rep. Lewis's office without an appointment, hoping I might have a chance to at least say hello. His assistant at the front desk went back to check if he was available and mentioned that I was a student at Fisk University, where he had graduated. Moments later Rep. John Lewis walked out with warmth and hospitality and welcomed me in. He showed me the pictures that hung on his Congressional office walls from his time in the movement. With each picture, he told the story and named the names. "That's Hezekiah Watkins, do you know his story?" or "This is in Selma," as we made our way around. I was there learning for an hour. It was such a rich time and experience, one that I hold onto.

Finally, before I left, we walked over to his desk and Rep. Lewis said, "You'll appreciate this," and opened a drawer.

He pulled out a framed document for me to look at. "This is my arrest certificate from Nashville." He kept it framed in his desk as a reminder. From the Nashville jail to Congress.

And here I was, waiting outside the new Nashville jail downtown when I heard the news of his passing. It was heavy. I didn't grasp the grief at the time.

"Mercy," was the only word that came out. "This loss is hard."

It's hard to lose our personal heroes. It's hard to lose such lights and voices of wisdom in such a tumultuous time. John Lewis's last public appearance had been just a couple of weeks prior at Black Lives Matter Plaza in Washington, DC. His heart was always with young people and the movement.

I cried. I mourned. I questioned why our elders were passing as young people were rising up all across the nation for racial justice and civil rights.

Rev. Venita later told our group that "God was raising up new warriors, a new generation of freedom fighters, as the older warriors were laid to rest." This was a sacred time. A passing of the torch. We were not going to allow the legacies of John Lewis, C. T. Vivian, or any of our ancestors in the struggle to be whitewashed. The very same streets that we walked surrounding the Plaza were the streets they marched in the 1960s on the way to sit in at the downtown lunch counters.

One of the main churches where young civil rights activists had trained for the sit-ins, First Baptist Capitol Hill, was just a block away in the same area where many of us parked to walk up to the Plaza for our protests every day. The reminders were all around us, every moment and everywhere. "Pick up the torch and continue the struggle" was the message. "The Civil Rights Movement is not over."

FIGURE 10.8. March 23, 1963. Demonstrators march in the vicinity of the downtown area to protest racial discrimination in Nashville. Holding the "Join the Freedom March" sign is John Lewis, chairman of the Student Central Committee of the Nashville Christian Leadership Council, sponsors of the movement. Photo © Frank Empson / *The Tennessean* via Imagn Content Services.

The next day, Governor Bill Lee had the flag lowered outside the capitol for a statesman often referred to as "The Conscience of Congress." But for those of us sitting on the Plaza, this symbolic act did not seem to respect John Lewis's true legacy. It felt like an insult. How could the governor order the flag to be lowered outside when injustice was still happening inside? How could they claim to honor John Lewis while ordering mass arrests and defending police violence against activists? Throughout that summer, they had showed us how they would have treated young people like Lewis, sitting in and disrupting business as usual fifty years before. How could they claim to respect a man who dedicated his life's work to racial justice and

FIGURE 10.9. July 18, 2020. Protesters on the upper Plaza honor Rep. John Lewis with a banner celebrating "good trouble" the day after his death. Troopers were sent out an hour later to demand its removal. Photo by Ray Di Pietro.

still fight to maintain the power structures of white supremacy? This was not just an obvious dissonance; it is the very strategy of oppressive powers to co-opt our heroes and to celebrate them in death while opposing everything they stood for in life.

In response, those of us at the Plaza put up our own tribute to the legacy of John Lewis. Someone had printed a ten-foot paper banner with some of John Lewis's most famous words: "Good Trouble." It was hung on the gate surrounding the upper Plaza and was visible to us across the street and to everyone who drove by. This was our tribute and continued call to action. Not even an hour later, troopers were sent out to say it had to be removed.

Over the following days we continued to hold tributes and memorials for John Lewis and C. T. Vivian in the Plaza. It became a community grieving place, and many more community members showed up for vigil and remembrance. One of the Plaza artists created beautiful murals with portraits of John Lewis and C. T. Vivian. We kept candles lit there, and it became a space where people dropped off flowers. Some lawmakers and faith leaders showed up to speak at the vigils. Another young woman who sang and had become active with the Plaza that month opened up in song, with the words of "Rise Up" by Andra Day.

This was one of the few spaces of public grief and commemoration for our heroes at the time; it was also an activated and living memorial to continuing their work. We remained in the Plaza as a presence of hope and a constant reminder of the need for systemic transformation.

Periodic arrests continued, but mass arrests had halted since the ACLU lawyers sent their letter. The troopers remained much more aggressive about arresting individuals for chalk with felony charges. Surveillance tactics increased, and troopers became more visible and intentional in bringing out video cameras to record us. They continued to rip down signs and push people down or away.

On July 29, NewsChannel 5 published a story documenting the nearly $1 million in overtime spent to keep troopers stationed outside the capitol monitoring us. It was a waste of money spent by "fiscal conservative" Governor Bill Lee to avoid having conversations with his constituents. Money to avoid action on racial justice concerns.

We were in the Plaza for forty days. Then for fifty days. Still waiting for an answer. Waiting for a response.

On August 3, 2020, we got it.

FIGURE 10.10. August 1, 2020. Clarissa (right), Miles (left), and other protesters dance in the crosswalk between the Tennessee State Capitol and the Plaza in a day of celebration marking fifty days of the People's Plaza occupation. Photo by Ray Di Pietro.

Governor Lee announced that he was calling a special session, largely focused on targeting our protest activities outside the capitol. They meant to increase penalties and crack down even harder on the People's Plaza. They wanted to force us to leave for good. The administration was strategizing ways to have us removed, and also considering ways to expand the definition of "illegal camping" as an item for the special session.

Tennessee Speaker of the House Cameron Sexton released a statement that said, "I am very appreciative of the call to strengthen existing laws against those who deface property, who escalate peaceful protests into acts of aggression and those who seek violence towards law enforcement and judicial members."

None of this described us. It was a part of their narrative to portray us as criminals and to criminalize our protests and presence. They could not wear us down or intimidate us with troopers, so they went for the "scorched earth" option. If we would not leave, they would force us out with the power of the state and its mechanisms.

We went on full alert. This was a battle we had no idea how to win. How would we resist? Would they clear us out beforehand? The Plaza belonged to the People, but that reclamation made those in power feel threatened. They would do whatever it took to take it back. We would become a cautionary tale for others who refuse to bend. They would use their full weight to try and make us break.

The session was set for August 10.

II

Aggravated Littering

Governor Lee and the leadership in the legislature were coordinating the impending special session. It was clear that the decision had been made to pass the new anti-protest bills even before the session began. The rhetoric of "law and order," "chaos," and "stopping violence" pointed to the false narrative they had already created about our protests. We knew that. The special session was just a formality. Nonetheless, we also knew that we had to organize resistance and raise public awareness about what they were trying to do. We could not back down silently, we could not allow it to happen without raising dissent. They were going to make an example out of us—a deterrent for future long-term demonstrations outside the bounds of preapproved, permitted protests. We decided to resist as a way to make sure their politics of repression and harm did not operate in the comfort of silence.

Two anti-protest bills were filed. They were sponsored by House Majority Leader William Lamberth and Senate Majority Leader Jack Johnson:

> **HB8004** would give jurisdiction to the Attorney General
> to prosecute cases related to protests, allowing the

FIGURE 11.1. August 4, 2020. Woman arrested and charged with felony vandalism for writing Breonna Taylor's name in chalk on the bronze doors of the Capitol building. Multiple state troopers were sent out to arrest her as she peacefully complied and was taken to the downtown jail. Photo by Ray Di Pietro.

state to prosecute even if the District Attorney for the county declines.

HB8005 mandated a thirty-day incarceration period for someone who "knowingly causes physical contact" considered provocative or offensive with a law enforcement officer (including spitting);
allowed people to be charged with disorderly conduct or rioting even if they are not "present" at the scene;
expanded the definition of "camping" to include protest or occupation activities like storing food;
made "camping" by that definition a felony offense; and

required a twelve-hour hold for camping and vandalism
arrests before posting bond.

This was their response to over fifty days of our presence
in the Plaza. Rather than addressing the issues we had been out
there for—the crisis of racism and police brutality in Tennessee—
Governor Lee called a $200,000 special session to avoid speaking
to us. The special session would do nothing to help everyday
Tennesseans amid the ongoing pandemic; it was just more crimi-
nalization and abuse of power.

We called on the community to join us outside the capitol on that upcoming Monday to lift voices, to take action,
and to call on the lawmakers who would be coming back for
the special session to stop their policy violence. We shared
informational graphics, sent emails, encouraged people to call
legislative offices directly, and prepared for a week of action
outside the capitol.

Things soon disintegrated. With so many moving parts, a
rushed timeline, and confusion about what was going to happen next, the situation grew tense with uncertainty and anxiety.
Fear pervaded the Plaza. At our General Assembly meetings
over the next few days, discussions about leaving became much
more prevalent and pronounced.

People were tired and traumatized. Exhaustion was real.
There was a genuine concern that the troopers would resume
raids to clear out the Plaza before lawmakers arrived as a pre-
emptive measure to keep us from protesting or disrupting the
meetings. Time and time again, the governor and his troopers
had shown they wanted to get rid of us. This would be their
chance to unleash everything they had left.

FIGURE 11.2. August 3, 2020. One of the nightly People's Plaza General Assemblies held in the shadow of the Tennessee State Capitol building. This was the main decision-making process for the group and a place for announcements and discussions on the ever-evolving needs of the protest. Photo by Ray Di Pietro.

We had been out there nearly two months straight, and the compounded traumas of what we had all experienced could not be avoided. As we discussed strategy, some people proposed leaving as a way to make sure we had numbers and weren't swept away by mass raids before the session even began. They thought strategically it would also help challenge the governor's narrative of "lawlessness" if we abided and did not stay through the night. The proposal was presented to leave the night before the special session and show up the next day to protest.

After all that we had faced and endured, many of us who had been there since the Plaza's early days objected. The purpose of staying out in the first place, openly defying the risk of "unlawful camping" orders and the governor's threats, was non-cooperation with unjust laws. We were tired of cycles of protest that would pop up and retreat to normalcy. We were tired of protests that were restricted to certain areas and permit mandates; a "permitted protest" was nothing more than a parade. The purpose of our demonstration was disruption. It was for those in power to see us daily and to be reminded through our constant and visible presence of the issues we recognized as an emergency.

The People's Plaza had been out there for over fifty days straight. We had been steadfast and unmovable. If we allowed the governor's bullying to move us before the special session even began, we would cede our moral clarity as to why we were there in the first place.

Still, others rose up and said it was time to go, that they were effectively done and this was the wisest exit strategy.

The meeting went on for hours. Discussions grew tense. There were valid points made on both sides. We took a vote. It was August 8, 2020. The majority voted to leave and end the nonstop sit-in on the Plaza. The plan was to resume in the daytime during the special sessions as an alternative form of protests.

This was hard. Those of us who felt the need to stay huddled and regrouped. Rev. Venita said she felt this was like "the battle of Gideon's army and we couldn't surrender" but needed to keep fighting with the remnant of folks who remained. Niti said she felt spiritually we were giving up right at the precipice of all that summer's labor. Mohamed and others shared their desire to hold the space and hold our ground. Another protester who had been there since the first day was in to stay. Terry was back and ready to keep going. Another spoke the words he always did, a constant reminder in the Plaza: "This is spiritual, right."

We couldn't leave yet, and we told some of the other folks who had been helping organize about our gut instinct to stay. They said the group had already decided and were leaving, but they would leave a few canopies for those few of us who decided to remain.

That was all we needed. We stayed.

The day before the special session, Sunday, August 9, we decided to use as a day of regrounding and what Martin Luther King Jr. described as the step of "self-purification" prior to nonviolent action. We wore white and sat under the canopies sharing stories and experiences that centered us ahead of the brewing storm.

Incense was burned around the Plaza. New art and colorful cloths were put up. Readings were shared from the diversity of faiths many of us represented: Hindu, Muslim, Christian, Jewish, and those who did not ascribe to a particular faith but believed in our collective good and a universal force for justice. Some of us fasted until sunset. Niti's mother brought large containers of homemade Indian food to break our fast. It was a calming time that helped bring down collective anxiety and refocus us.

We stayed through the night and others came to join us. One of those who stopped by that night was State Representative Gloria Johnson, who had just driven into town from Knoxville for the special session and wanted to stop by the Plaza to offer words of support. We continued to hold the Plaza that night. The troopers watched from across the street. There were about a dozen of us there, so it would have been easy for them to raid, but we weren't afraid. As it grew later, we talked, sat around, and some folks lay on the ground. Some played music to keep spirits high and others teased them about their song selections. We were together, no matter what the next day's session would bring.

On the morning of August 10, 2020, as the special session began, more folks showed up to line the streets holding signs. I hurried home to change and brush my teeth. We had stayed up most of the night and were running on adrenaline. Many more folks showed up throughout the day. A couple hundred people were present by the afternoon. Dozens of cars participated in a honk-a-thon that circled the capitol building. Car horns blared in a constant chorus as lawmakers came out to spectate on the balcony. We gathered outside on the upper Plaza with signs and drums.

A large group of us marched to the back gate where other members of the public were walking in to enter the special session as visitors. As we approached, a trooper quickly pulled the metal bike racks together and said we were not allowed inside.

"Why are we not allowed inside, when we just saw you let people in without an issue?" I asked.

"Yeah, you didn't even check their IDs or anything," someone shouted out.

The troopers just stood there silently.

"You're not allowed inside," was the only response given.

We congregated at the back gate. Rev. Venita and some of the other movement grandmothers who had shown up in person to join us that day—Jane Osgerby, Vivian Ervin, and Anna Grabowski—came to the front of the crowd, face-to-face with the troopers. Were they really going to block grandmothers from entering a public meeting in the capitol?

"Are we allowed in?" Miss Vivian asked a trooper.

The troopers were silent. One started radioing inside for assistance, even as more came out to line the barricades.

"In the name of my uncle that was killed fighting Nazis, I tell you to let us in this public meeting of our democracy," said Miss Anna, who had driven hours from rural East Tennessee to attend, as she stared at the troopers eye to eye.

After a few minutes, Sergeant Buchanan hung up his phone and stepped forward to address the crowd.

"If you've been incarcerated and arrested inside the capitol for disrupting, you're not allowed inside," he announced. "This directive is from the Speaker's Office. If you've been arrested you're not allowed inside."

Another arbitrary rule, and we knew exactly who it applied to.

"Furthermore," he went on, "only ten people are allowed inside."

This was ridiculous.

Speaker Cameron Sexton was giving orders to the troopers to keep the People out of the People's House. We wanted to know what was happening from witnesses inside, so ten people who hadn't been previously arrested went in to stand in the House gallery as representatives of the hundreds of us outside. No signs were allowed.

The rest of us waited for a while at the back gate. We continued to chant and sing.

"No justice!"

"No peace!"

"No racist!"

"Police!"

"Whose House?"

"Our House!"

FIGURE 11.3. August 10, 2020. Plaza protesters and state troopers surround the truck of State Senator Joey Hensley in front of the Tennessee State Capitol. Protesters are showing opposition to the anti-protest bills (which Hensley supports) being voted on in the legislature that week. Photo by Ray Di Pietro.

Our friends inside texted us updates. That first day, the session's business was brief. After mainly introductory comments and announcements, the lawmakers adjourned with plans to begin taking up the more substantive matters the next day in committees.

We marched to the legislative offices on the other side of Capitol Hill to stand outside the parking garage as lawmakers left for the day. Since we had not been allowed inside, we wanted to be sure they saw us and knew our opposition to the injustices that targeted our rights.

Dozens of us gathered with signs outside the parking garage; people overflowed onto the sidewalks and street. The crowd soon spread in front of the parking garage exit, where a line of legislators waited in their cars. A large group of troopers came out to push everyone back and clear the roads. As the space cleared, lawmakers began zooming out, some shaking their heads and making comments through their windows. They wouldn't talk to us. They didn't see us as human, just as a nuisance to avoid.

Those of us protesting spread out with our signs. I was crossing the street when I saw Representative Jerry Sexton driving out in a car recording us and laughing. I stopped in the street as troopers rushed forward around me.

"Arrest him," Lieutenant Michael Morgan yelled from a few feet away. I started to walk toward the sidewalk but was stopped by the trooper who told me I was under arrest.

Rep. G. A. Hardaway, who was walking, approached the trooper handcuffing me to get an explanation and see if I could be released since I was clearly walking to the sidewalk.

"Nope, he's under arrest. Talk to the Lieutenant," the trooper responded as he pushed me forward into the parking garage. At the time I was the only one arrested. People were chanting. As I passed by, I handed my phone to Dragon from behind my back. I asked him to call Niti. We walked the long underground tunnel to the capitol basement for the troopers to fill out paperwork.

I was charged with "obstructing a highway or passageway" and then brought to jail. It was still mid-afternoon. A few hours later, a protester who had helped with our safety team since our first weeks at the Plaza was arrested as well. He said there was an incident with Senator Joey Hensley threatening to run people over. People had been standing in the street holding signs outside the capitol and continuing to lift their voices in protest. The troopers had continued to push people back and clear the roads.

He and I were the only two arrested that day. I called Niti for updates on bail and release. She said the jail was having an issue with my paperwork. Hours later the other protester was released, but they were still having issues with my paperwork. It was getting later. I began to anticipate another trip upstairs.

Finally, Niti got word from the night magistrate about what was going on. The magistrate had called to check with the jail, since I had not even been able to go through that part of the process yet. Apparently the trooper who arrested me had forgotten to turn in the paperwork. So I was stuck there. This had not happened before. Niti called legal support, but she wasn't able to get through to any lawyers that night. I was stuck.

She then tried one last idea: reaching out to State Representative Mike Stewart. Rep. Stewart had been a consistent support at the Plaza and had come down periodically to join us as a Nashville-based legislator to observe. He was preparing for the next day's session as Niti explained my situation. As a lawyer, he offered to help and came down to the night magistrate's office with his Tennessee Bar Association card in hand to seek my release. Ultimately, the magistrate got in touch with the trooper's commanders and let them know that if the paperwork was not turned over in the next couple of hours he would release me. It was around midnight and the arresting trooper was already at home, but he returned and got the paperwork in. My bail was paid, and I was released.

We returned to the Plaza for another night. Most of the crowds had gone home with plans to return the next day. We ate. We talked. All of us were exhausted. A couple people stayed up through the night keeping watch, but not me; I fell asleep sitting in a chair.

In the morning, protests resumed. Crowds returned to hold signs and the honk-a-thon continued.

In the afternoon, a few of us were allowed to testify virtually before the Senate Committee about our opposition to the anti-protest bills. We testified via livestream from our phones, sitting right outside the capitol, engaged in the very act of protest that the bills being proposed sought to stop.

"This bill would further divide our state," Rev. Venita testified before the committee. "You all are elected to preserve the future of this state. If our state government can look at these young protesters as the next generation crying out for change, rather than seeking ways to arrest them for signs and chalk, and to silence their voices, we can build a greater state."

Dede West, Anjanette Edwards, and I testified as well. State Senator Janice Bowling was the only member to ask a question.

"What exactly are the changes you're demanding?"

"Number one, we need to demilitarize the troopers," Rev. Venita responded. "What we have witnessed over the last sixty days is intimidation, children being chased down streets, being provoked, and these are young people . . . they are all of our children crying out for change. So they're asking for the demilitarizing of the police. We have unjust penal systems and prison systems that are harshly against a race of people. We have poor housing conditions, poor health insurance. And these children are saying we want everybody to have a fair share . . . And obviously the legislators need some help at this."

They dismissed us, and the bill sailed through the committee without much discussion.

Outside, we continued to rally on the Plaza as the honk-a-thon encircled the capitol in protest. At one point a few lawmakers came out to heckle. State Representatives Jeremy Faison, Bruce Griffey, and Terri Lynn Weaver came out to stand at the railing on the upper Plaza with a large banner they had printed saying "Honk for Trump." It was all just a cruel joke for them. Representative Faison pushed Miss Ruth back as she held a picture of George Floyd, blocking it with the banner and laughing. Some of the troopers stood nearby watching all this and smirking.

That whole day was chaotic. The bill cruised through committees in both chambers of the legislature over the course of a day of discussions. As lawmakers left for the day, we returned to the parking garage with signs to meet them as they left. Dozens of troopers were already stationed there to make sure we did not get too close or block the exit. They continually came out to move people back. Most of the lawmakers rushed out, looking straight forward to avoid eye contact.

Rep. Gloria Johnson was one of the few who actually came out to stand and talk with us. She was one of the few who was not afraid of hearing from people about our concerns and frustrations about the bills being rammed through.

Troopers made more arrests later that day. One was a man from Chattanooga who had attended the protests for the first time. They accused him of throwing a plastic water bottle and tackled him to the ground. A few Plaza members went to the jail to get updates on his charge and status for legal support.

As it grew darker, the rest of us who had planned to spend the night returned to the canopies at the Plaza. Another day. Completely exhausted, I lay down on the granite steps and fell asleep on a backpack full of books, totally unaware of what was going on.

"Justin, Justin, wake up. Justin."

Niti was tapping me and trying to get me awake. Apparently other people had already tried, but I was just so tired I slept through it.

"Justin, it's an emergency," Niti said.

"What's going on?" I said, sitting up on the steps, still half-asleep.

One of the Plaza organizers who was coordinating jail support was at the magistrate's office when troopers came by to get another warrant.

"The warrant matches your Social Security number. It's for you," she said.

Another warrant. I had no idea what it was for or why it was so late. I was too tired.

"If they want to get me, I'm just going to stay here. No point in running," I said, lying back down.

In the morning, I called my lawyer and told him about the warrant update.

"I'll just go turn myself in," I said.

The thing about having a warrant hanging over my head was that the troopers had the power to stop and arrest me whenever they wanted. It was part of their plan to remove me before the vote on the bills as a way to keep me away from the protests.

Do not underestimate your opponent.

Rather than wait for them to take me whenever they pleased or planned, I went down to the Metro Nashville Police Department Warrants Division to turn myself in. I gave the officer at the desk my photo ID and information.

"I was told I have a warrant," I said as he ran my name in the system. He looked at it on the computer and then silently stepped away to make a phone call.

"Just have a seat," he said.

After about twenty minutes he returned. He looked a little confused.

"You have a warrant for aggravated littering," he told me. He hadn't seen this type of warrant before.

"For littering," I replied.

"Yes, but because of COVID-19 guidelines and the fact that it's a nonviolent offense, my supervisor directed me to give you a citation." He handed me a piece of paper. "Your court date is on there and you have to go to the court for booking as well."

I took the paper. It was all so perplexing. I was told to keep the paper on my person just in case the troopers decided to arrest me, to show them that I had already turned myself in.

I returned to the Plaza for the third and final day of the session. We rallied outside and continued the honk-a-thon as the lawmakers voted to pass HB8005.

HB8004, taking away the local district attorney's jurisdiction in protest-related offenses, was not moved forward, as an agreement appeared to be reached between DA Glenn Funk and the Republicans in the legislature. What the agreement was, we didn't know.

That afternoon, my lawyer called me to let me know that the DA had filed a motion to alter my bond conditions, banning me from the capitol grounds and requiring GPS monitoring. Coincidence? It did not appear so. This motion was filed in tandem with the removal of the bill stripping the DA's power. It appeared I was the compromise. My court hearing was set for the next day.

FIGURE II.4. August 12, 2020. Plaza protesters stand at barricades on the upper Plaza facing the capitol. This space was closed and then reopened in the ever-shifting rule changes of the Plaza space. These barricades marked another barrier that would result in arrest for criminal trespassing if crossed. State troopers kept guard on the other side. Photo by Ray Di Pietro.

As the vote was taken, we took to the streets to get around the Plaza. Some folks chained themselves to the upper Plaza railing in an act of protest. It was hot and chaotic. As the honk-a-thon continued around the capitol, the troopers had started pulling people over and giving them tickets. Lawmakers kept coming out to the balconies, pointing and making comments.

Mohamed and I were stopped down the street as we stepped out of the car to record. The trooper said we "ran a red light," but after writing down Mohamed's license plate and VIN number, he and his backup left without giving a ticket.

Protests continued on the Plaza. Anger, hurt, and weariness were audible in the chants. The intent of the bill was to deter people from protesting, yet there we were.

HB8005 passed through the supermajority legislature. The governor and legislative leaders held a press conference, a victory lap. Being out there on the Plaza would effectively now become a felony offense. Those chained to the railing were arrested later that night. The handcuffs they had used to attach themselves were snapped with bolt cutters. They were charged with "criminal trespassing." On public property.

It was over.

From June 12, 2020, to August 12, 2020, we had remained outside on the Plaza, and now it was time to leave. We were tired. We had endured and held the space through the special session that made our presence a felony. Our resistance had not broken, but it was time to reassess and restrategize. How would our fight evolve?

I went home that night and slept in my own bed. I fell asleep thinking, "What more could they do to us?" The next morning I had to prepare for my court appearance on the DA's motion.

The governor, the troopers, the prosecutors, and the lawmakers had all worked in tandem to shut us down. The People's Plaza was an act of protest, but it had also become a symbol of something they wanted to censor and erase. The passage of such an extreme anti-protest law was confirmation that our continual act of protest had significance. Our presence there was not in vain. It meant something—otherwise they wouldn't have fought so hard to stop us.

State of Tennessee
vs. Justin Jones

"Autonomous zones will not be tolerated."

That was the warning Governor Lee had given us the day we reclaimed the Plaza for the People on June 12, 2020. At the time, we had no idea what his threat would come to mean. They tried every measure, every use of force, every intimidation tactic they could devise and yet, months later, we had remained.

After those sixty-two days, I was ready to rest. I was ready to stay in bed. I was ready to breathe. But the next morning I had to wake up early to go to court for the district attorney's motion. The Plaza sit-in was officially over, but their motion to ban me from capitol grounds and require GPS monitoring remained.

After a brief walk around the neighborhood with Denali, I put on my blue suit and tie. I hadn't worn anything like that all summer. I didn't have time for breakfast, and I was too anxious to be hungry. I drank some tea and rushed to court.

Nick was there, ready with his response on my behalf. He hadn't seen anything like this. District Attorney Funk had assigned one of his office's top prosecutors to my case. Niti,

Mohamed, Rev. Venita, and Rep. Hardaway were also there for moral support and as potential witnesses.

What compelling evidence would be presented that warranted such an extreme restriction of my constitutional rights? GPS monitoring? The hearing had even been expedited with an emergency motion from the DA's office. What was the urgency?

I arrived in court and sat at the table on the defense side.

Court has a strange power dynamic. It is unsettling, every single time, to hear the clerk read off *People of the State of Tennessee vs. Justin Jones*, no matter how many court dates I've had. Which people? The prosecution and this targeted motion did not represent the people I knew, or those whom I had come to know in the Plaza.

The prosecutor began his case. The urgency of this request stemmed from the state's position that I was an "increasing threat to public safety." That was the basis of their motion. The prosecutor listed off the numerous times I had been arrested that summer and the various charges, including the most recent for "aggravated littering." It all started to make more sense. That's why they had sought that warrant for such a petty offense. It was all a part of a strategy; the warrant and motion to revoke my bond were coordinated efforts. Do not underestimate your opponent.

We had kept the Plaza clean. We had provided our own sanitation supplies. We had routinely swept and mopped and removed garbage. Littering was a stretch.

The prosecution called their first and only witness. A trooper. Lieutenant Michael Morgan.

Lt. Morgan walked in and sat at the witness stand after taking the oath to tell the truth. As the prosecutor started asking questions, Lt. Morgan went into a monologue about how he had seen me protesting at the capitol for the past few years and how my tactics were becoming more "violent and extreme."

"I have seen a shift in Justin," he told the judge.

He said I had assaulted him and other troopers. No video or other evidence of these accusations was presented. Just Lt. Morgan's testimony. Lt. Michael Morgan is the same trooper who had a complaint filed against him in 2018 for placing an African American man in a chokehold at a protest at the capitol. All the violent labels—from "assault" to "rioting"—that the state tried to lay on us were just projections of their own behavior.

After the state presented its case, my lawyer called Niti as a witness to testify about what she had seen that summer. She explained to the judge that we were nonviolent, that she had been present most of the summer and never witnessed me assault anyone as the trooper suggested. We were engaged in nonviolent direct action. In return, we were terrorized emotionally and physically.

After both sides had presented, the prosecutor and my lawyer moved to closing arguments.

The prosecutor reiterated that the motion was in the interest of public safety. I was a "threat" to the safety of lawmakers and the public. Nick followed with a direct response to all the accusations.

"Yes, Justin is a threat," he said. "He is a threat to the good ol' boys network and way of doing things. That is what this motion is about."

He went on to uplift Nashville's civil rights legacy and the tradition of "good trouble" as exemplified by activists like John Lewis and Diane Nash. This motion was antithetical to everything we claimed to represent as a city and society seeking greater justice. Nick did not hold back. He spoke words that made clear this motion was bigger than me individually. It was about silencing our movement. It was about retaliation. It was about power systems feeling threatened and needing to lash out.

After listening to both sides, the judge was prepared to make his ruling. He had been stoic for the most part, and I was nervous to hear his thoughts.

After considering the motion and evidence presented, he said he rejected the state's request.

"If granted," said the judge, "the motion would set a slippery slope when it comes to monitoring the right to free movement even before someone has had the opportunity to have a trial."

I was so relieved. Lt. Morgan, red-faced, stormed past us and out of the court. I thanked my lawyer and then went out to thank Niti, Mohamed, Rev. Venita, and Rep. Hardaway. It was a day of victory after the anti-protest bill passing just the day before, which had left some of us feeling defeated.

That's how every day that summer felt, like a pendulum moving back and forth between celebration and defeat. Up and down. Backward and forward. I guess that's the nature of our struggle.

That whole summer, for sixty-two days, we had spent our time fighting a power that we could not see. The extent of its reach and the layers of its depths were beyond what I had initially imagined. At the beginning—despite the best of advice—I had underestimated our opposition, from the governor's office, troopers, local police, and Republican lawmakers, to the Democratic district attorney.

They control every aspect of our state. It took me two months to realize that, according to their metrics, we are "powerless." It is impossible to beat them at a game in which they control the rules and determine who wins and who loses.

So what difference does it make to continually put our bodies in the mix, to be arrested and brutalized by state violence? How long will we simply be fibers ground up by the cogs of the machine? It is evil, and we have to resist it.

These were some of the thoughts I had over the weeks after the end of the Plaza. But then I was reminded of the power in relationships formed, the new people brought into the movement who had never been involved before, and the power in our presence, which made the state use every tool at its disposal to try to crush us.

There is power in sitting in and reclaiming public space.

The following month I took a road trip across the country, to California, to visit family. It was a necessary escape. I had to process.

I got to visit with my Lola, my maternal grandmother. I remember one night after I had been there about a week, my Lola came to talk to me late as I was preparing for sleep. We had often talked when I called from jail, as her phone number was one of the few I knew from memory. She wanted to show me something. We walked into her bedroom where she had an altar and candle set up. With tears in her eyes she hugged me and pointed to the candle.

"You see the candle," she said. "Every day you were out there, sixty-two days, I kept a candle lit for you. Praying for you. Praying for you to be safe."

We sat down, cried, and exhaled.

Conclusion

*Remember what we are doing is important. We are
doing this for generations yet unborn.*

DIANE NASH

I just spoke with a group of young adults who are learning about
community organizing and building collective power through
a Bay Area–based nonprofit. I talked to them about the Plaza. I
shared some of what we witnessed, what we experienced, the
trauma, the joy, and how the struggle continues. Mental health
came up—how the harm continues to impact many of us, not
just overtly in ongoing charges and court dates, but also emotionally, psychologically, and spiritually. It is a harm that persists.

The Plaza occupation is over a year in the past now. It is a
living memory. Writing this book, I have had to revisit and relive
those experiences numerous times—moments good and bad,
moments that make me smile, and moments full of horror.

On June 23, 2021, I found myself back in the Nashville jail.
District Attorney Glenn Funk indicted me on two new charges
stemming from our time in the Plaza. Going to a site of harm is
never easy. The process of being handcuffed, taking mugshots,
and waiting were like déjà vu. Almost a year to the day of us

FIGURE 13.1. July 23, 2021. Justin leaves a courtroom surrounded by elders and community members after the judge dismisses another of his fourteen charges. In this case, troopers had falsely accused him of assaulting an officer with a megaphone during the Plaza protest. The charge was proved false when Trooper Asa Pearl brought in a blue megaphone that he said was used in the alleged assault, even though the megaphone Justin had that evening was red. The trooper and prosecutor later explained that this was a "mix-up." Photo by Ray Di Pietro.

beginning our Plaza occupation, DA Funk had gone before the grand jury in a secret process to obtain an indictment on two charges of "reckless endangerment."

The charges stemmed from an incident on June 18, 2020, when a truck pushed its way through protesters in the street outside the capitol. Protesters were standing in the street right after the troopers had raided us again. The white male driver was not charged, but I was charged with endangering him for tossing a rubber traffic cone in front of the truck as he pushed his way through. The troopers had located the man and convinced him to file charges months after he initially declined to do so. The district attorney was under pressure to bring additional charges against me, because the other twelve were not sticking in court. It was a coordinated and calculated act.

Including these indictments, I faced a total of fourteen criminal charges from the summer of the People's Plaza. Despite all the recorded instances of police brutality, only one state trooper ever faced charges: Trooper Harvey Briggs, for a viral video of him ripping the mask off a protester. On the other hand, Plaza protesters were arrested over two hundred times, on charges that have mostly been thrown out or dismissed in court.

At various points while writing this book, I have had to pause to take a step back. Certain things were triggered in me, things that I did not even know were lodged in my being, things that had gone unaddressed. While traumatic events are unfolding and escalating, it is difficult to think about how you are being impacted. In my case, it started to show up months later in the forms of anxiety and depression.

I share this to say that *The People's Plaza* is a testimony that I offer as one member, one voice, one witness among many. There are so many stories from sixty-two days, twenty-four hours a day, that it would be impossible to share everything. Many of our folks are still dealing with repercussions and lasting wounds—visible and invisible. We must tell the story together.

Because we are now at a crossroads.

On January 6, 2021, the nation watched packs of angry white Americans storm the US Capitol in an act of insurrection. It showed us another side of the white supremacist destruction that threatens the safety and well-being of our communities.

Watching it unfold live on the news, like many, I felt shock but not disbelief. All signs had pointed to this. All the rhetoric from the white power structure had made clear that there would not be a peaceful transition of administrations. That there would be a backlash. It is a routine ritual of racism. This was the shadow of America showing itself once again, not lurking in the undercurrent as always, but out in the open and broadcast live. Unashamed. Unmasked. No longer in white sheets, but in red Make America Great Again hats, Proud Boy polos, 1776 t-shirts, waving American flags.

The same arrogant privilege of white supremacy that led Derek Chauvin to murder George Floyd—believing he was outside the bounds of the law because of his badge and his whiteness—was now trying to choke the already faint breath out of our democracy.

As the insurrectionists broke through the first barricades and started charging toward the US Capitol, I watched intently, waiting for hundreds of law enforcement officers to descend upon them, surround them, and make mass arrests. Surely this would happen—it had happened to us for much less. Just months earlier in Nashville, state troopers had not hesitated to violently "defend" our empty state capitol from us—a group of unarmed young people gathered on a public plaza with paper signs and songs. I had experienced firsthand how quickly militarized police forces and the National Guard could be mobilized and deployed against us in our own community.

Where were they now? Where was their "law and order"? Where were their condemnations of rioting and violence? Where was the blue line?

The insurrectionists continued to make their way up to the Capitol, climbing walls, breaking windows, parading inside, making death threats. On the lawn, they had erected a gallows with a noose. They pushed against the officers who finally arrived. Other officers acted as accomplices and waved them in. A purge was happening. It was like hell had opened up and let loose all the bile that had been metastasizing in America's feeble soul. It was a sickness we saw take hold and explode before our very eyes.

What an utterly different response they received than we did. We were not trying to overturn our democracy. We were not attempting to take politicians hostage. We were rounded up, arrested, and brutalized for saying that our lives matter. That Black Lives Matter. For calling our state government and this nation to a higher ground. January 6, 2021, was about terrorism and destruction; our protests in the summer of 2020 were rooted in redemption and reckoning. We sought reparation of a broken society, rejection of racialized state terror, and reconstruction to ensure a better future for our children.

Despite all this, the Plaza remains a point in time I look back on with hope. It is a reminder of another way—an alternative path for both Tennessee and the nation. I have taken some time in the year since for introspection and reflection. Like so many of us in the movement, I have reckoned with the too-familiar questions: What is next? Where do we go from here?

The work must continue, even as it evolves. News and social media can easily flood us with such a litany of overwhelming disasters that we find it hard to focus. We might even freeze or burn out. How do we deal with trauma that only seems to be compounding? We are now dealing with the backlash to 2020's mass racial justice movement, in the form of policies aimed at further criminalizing protest (such as increased penalties, and immunity for drivers who run over protesters) and others trying to enact bans on teaching about systemic racism and history in

our schools. In Tennessee, these are the policies we saw priori-
tized in the 2021 legislative session.

It is apparent now, more than ever, that it was not our actions
that were deemed threatening—we conducted ourselves according to the tactics of nonviolent confrontation. What was dangerous was our message and what we represented. That is what
the power structures sought to stomp out. If our being there
did not mean something, the state would not have plotted and
schemed so relentlessly to repress us. They would not have
worked in literal overtime to wipe us out of the way. This is the
power that we recognized and retook—People Power—that the
state leaders feared so much.

How dare we come together as a multiracial group in the
façade of state authority, disrupting the status quo? How dare
we try to practice what democracy and justice can be on the
steps of a building that shamelessly misappropriates those values? How dare we engage in mutual aid and collective care,
spotlighting the poverty that plagues our community? How dare
we reclaim dead public space and give it new meaning and life?
How dare we have the audacity not to be broken? How dare
we no longer fear their jails and arbitrary laws? How dare we
continue to have joy in the face of their oppression as we resist?
How dare we remain there for sixty-two days?

The coordination of the governor, Republican lawmakers,
and Tennessee state troopers to break us, crush us, and silence
us cannot be dismissed. We were meant to be made an example
of, so that others would not put a mirror to the racist face of the
capitol. Imagine the money spent, almost $2 million to pay troop-
ers overtime to wage war against us as if we were enemy com-
batants, the myriad of frivolous charges that wasted resources
and only further exposed the inhumanity of our jail systems.

What our movement and so many others faced during the racial justice uprisings in the summer of 2020 is normalized as we consider our nation's history—but it can never be called normal. The overreactions of the state government and its militarized police force, the mass arrests, documented surveillance, and weaponization of the legal system are violence and nothing less. And as in all cases of violence perpetuated by the state throughout time, the trauma inflicted upon us has not been redressed. It lives on in our bodies and psyches. Nightmares not easily forgotten. Writing this book, I have often wondered if the troopers, jail guards, and politicians struggle with the same. Are they proud that violence is their legacy? Will they be honest with their children and grandchildren about where they stood in this time? Or will they defend their actions as "just following orders"? I know only history can answer these questions, so I offer this testimony for the record.

The People's Plaza is a movement of mostly young people and the houseless community, literally risen from the margins of power, from the grassy fringe of what they call Legislative Plaza. Those rejected by white supremacist society, those dismissed as naïve, those ignored by racist, normative powers, the inexperienced, the poor, the young—these were the Plaza's peaceful occupants. We inverted the values of state power and created a new paradigm that demanded a reaction.

We didn't wait for them to rename the Legislative Plaza . . . we renamed it for Ida B. Wells. We didn't heed their warnings not to spend the night on the capitol grounds . . . we did it for sixty-two days. We renewed and purified Capitol Hill in Nashville with our songs, cries, prayers, sweat, and art. We gave it a new purpose and meaning for our community. We breathed new life into its dry bones. And in so doing we found our own purpose.

I heard multiple times that the Plaza was a place of acceptance and family, particularly for those who felt rejected because of their race, sexuality, or financial status. It was a place where people could be their authentic selves. A few of the young people who came and joined us as allies were kicked out of their homes by conservative parents who condemned them for participating in the protests. The Plaza created a sacred space of welcome, belonging, and resistance. I see now that this is what drew people from all walks of life to put their bodies on the line time after time, despite brutality and abuse by state forces. One young Black brother who joined us—and often led our protest chants by keeping rhythm for us on the drums—told me how the Plaza had given him purpose. Struggling with addiction, he told me one night, as we sat under the canopies, that rediscovering that purpose saved his life.

"I have never been a part of anything like this before," he told me. "I love y'all for that."

He said he hoped it never ended.

We as a generation are being summoned in this moment. Maybe it looks different than the protests of our past. We had on t-shirts, shorts, and jeans rather than suits and dress clothes. Folks had dyed hair, colorful tattoos, and our music was different. The Plaza even had a smoking section. We had yoga, interfaith services, and healing group therapy circles, and Niti led participants in a traditional Indian dance class. We are more open about our mental health, and we talk about such things without stigma. We had social media to amplify our message. We are picking up the torch and continuing the struggle in our own unique way, while still honoring the lineage of freedom fighters before us.

The friends and comrades I met in the Plaza give me hope. Our presence offered an alternative vision to that of the insurrectionists and their allies in government. The Plaza was a glimpse of another way. For me, the Plaza was a place of stark clarity, confirmation of what our generation is actively discovering to be our mission. This is a moment in which so much is on the line—and we may not get another chance. As systems fail and collapse all around us, we are tasked with both dismantling the broken and building something new. Something real. Something redemptive. Something that affirms our dignity and allows our children to flourish.

The Plaza is not just a physical space. The Plaza is inside us everywhere we go when we do so with a commitment to uplift those pushed to the margins and to build a multiracial democracy. The Plaza is a world refashioned, reformed, renamed.

The Plaza belongs to the People.

OCTOBER 14, 2021

Sixty-Two Days
at the People's Plaza

JUNE 12

- 5 p.m. Protesters gather at the Legislative Plaza on Capitol Hill
- Governor Bill Lee announces, "Autonomous zones will not be tolerated."

JUNE 13

- March for Justice in Legislative Plaza
- Tennessee Highway Patrol (THP) troopers push people off the upper Plaza to "power wash"
- Standoff with troopers on grass by Plaza until late at night
- First raid by troopers

JUNE 14

- Protesters move to the lower Plaza (across the street); set up canopies, tables, etc.

JUNE 15

- Moral Monday March led by faith leaders; confrontation with line of troopers who say people are not allowed in capitol despite legislative session

- First arrest: Terry arrested for disorderly conduct; she gets a black eye from being pushed down stairs by trooper and goes to hospital
- Evening. Twenty-one arrested when people refuse to leave upper Plaza; almost all cited and charged with illegal camping

JUNE 16

- Morning session in the Tennessee House gallery
- Ashanti Posey vote: GOP refuses to pass resolution in honor of Black Nashville teen killed by gun violence because of reports alleging she smoked marijuana
- Rep. Antonio Parkinson yells at Speaker Cameron Sexton on the House floor
- Three protesters arrested and charged with disrupting a public meeting and disorderly conduct; Jones is additionally charged with "assaulting" officer Lt. Michael Morgan

JUNE 17

- Second raid by troopers: THP confiscates water, canopies, medications, and personal belongings from demonstrators
- Ashanti Posey's mother joins protest at Ida B. Wells Plaza, honoring daughter who Tennessee lawmakers refused to honor in death

JUNE 18

- Midday. Third raid by troopers: water, canopies, personal belongings confiscated
- Five arrested for camping on state property, three arrested for criminal trespassing

JUNE 19

- Juneteenth mass protest as people try to get onto the Plaza
- Three hundred people pushed back from the Plaza by troopers; one trooper uses pepper spray
- National Guard deployed on front line to hold people back with shields and riot gear
- That evening, first "General Assembly" mass meeting held on Plaza steps, which would become the main decision-making process moving forward

JUNE 22

- Troopers remove protest signs
- Dozens of troopers sent to intimidate protesters
- Standoff between protesters and troopers on the grass

JUNE 23

- Another standoff on the grass ensues as protesters reclaim Ida B. Wells Plaza and demonstrators force troopers up to the capitol's doors
- Later in the day, troopers steal protest signs and use unnecessary force on the protesters
- Sergeant John Grinder pushes two houseless community members, plus Jonelle Christopher and Jones, as he bulldozes his way through protesters
- Sergeant Grinder is taken away by his colleagues
- Ambulance called to the scene to inspect an injured Tamara

JUNE 25

- 6:30 a.m. Troopers raid Ida B. Wells Plaza again: THP seizes community donations, signs, chairs, and personal

items of the houseless population, including their
medicines and canopies

JUNE 26
- Jones arrested for "inciting a riot" (dismissed) and
  "criminal trespass" around 10:15 p.m. (the capitol closes
  to the public at 11 p.m.)

JUNE 28
- "Back the Badge" counterprotest rally
- Forty-four People's Plaza protesters arrested for criminal
  trespassing for setting foot on Capitol Hill
- Excessive force used against Miss Ruth Reeves; a trooper
  puts his hand in Ruth's mouth to control her movements
- Another protester arrested and zip-tied so tightly that the
  troopers themselves have a hard time removing the ties;
  injuries documented

JUNE 29
- Troopers commence a morning raid
- Five people arrested

JUNE 30
- One protester arrested for "trespassing" on Capitol Hill

JULY 1
- Early morning. Troopers surround Ida B. Wells Plaza,
  flashing lights and blasting sirens to harass protesters
- Gov. Bill Lee calls for a meeting of the Capitol
  Commission for the following week on the removal
  of Nathan Bedford Forrest bust

JULY 4

- Mass protests at the Plaza with Teens for Equality group; people are dragged down the stairs
- Mass arrests for being on upper Plaza, which was arbitrarily closed
- Thirty-one demonstrators are arrested by the end of the day

JULY 9

- Tennessee Capitol Commission votes to remove Nathan Bedford Forrest bust

JULY 11

- Troopers rush crowd gathered at back of Capitol Hill without warning and arrest protesters
- Sen. Jeff Yarbro is there to witness

JULY 12

- One-month celebration on the Plaza
- Jones arrested on criminal warrant from previous day
- Standoff with troopers on the Plaza following Jones's release
- Troopers announce that anyone who spends the night will be arrested
- Demonstrators remain

JULY 14

- Protesters arrested for writing with chalk

JULY 16

- Ida B. Wells's birthday: celebration and art on the Plaza

JULY 17

- C. T. Vivian and John Lewis pass away

JULY 18

- Community vigil on the Plaza for Vivian and Lewis

JULY 24

- Cherri Foytlin and Indigenous water protectors come in solidarity from Bayou Pipeline protests

JULY 27

- Protesters try to attend Gov. Lee's press conference at National Guard Armory
- Gillum Ferguson, Gov. Lee's press secretary, refuses to start as long as protesters are present; protesters are escorted out by National Guard / police

AUGUST 3

- Gov. Bill Lee calls for special session of anti-protest bills targeting Plaza protests

AUGUST 8

- Some protesters vote to leave / end occupation in light of the impending special session
- A smaller group chooses to stay and hold space through at least the end of the vote

AUGUST 10

- The special session of the Tennessee General Assembly begins
- Jones arrested for blocking road

AUGUST 12

- Warrant issued for Jones's arrest for "aggravated littering"
- District attorney files a motion banning Jones from the capitol and requiring GPS monitoring
- Tennessee General Assembly passes anti-protest laws
- Sixteen people arrested after handcuffing themselves to the Capitol Hill gate in protest against General Assembly vote
- Plaza occupation ends

AUGUST 13

- Prosecution presents motion and says Jones is a "threat to public safety"
- Judge denies district attorney's motion on grounds that it is a slippery slope

Notes

CHAPTER I

7   **I got a call from Rev. Venita Lewis.** Only first names have been
     used when specifically requested, and in some cases names have
     been omitted to respect the privacy and anonymity of various
     Plaza participants.

CHAPTER 6

58   **They got paid overtime just to stand there.** Levi Ismail, "Millions
     Spent on Overtime for THP Troopers Guarding Capitol during
     Protests," NewsChannel 5 Nashville, September 24, 2020, https://
     www.newschannel5.com/news/millions-spent-on-overtime-for-
     thp-troopers-guarding-capitol-during-protests.

61   **Or were they going to kettle people in.** Kettling is a tactic often
     used by police, including the Tennessee Highway Patrol, at pro-
     tests; it's also known as "trap and detain." It involves a large force
     of officers surrounding individuals or groups from various points
     to corral them before making mass arrests.

CHAPTER 7

67   **Casada and his chief of staff, Cade Cothren, were forced to
     resign.** Natalie Allison and Adam Tamburin, "Special Prosecutor
     to Review Activist's Case after Questions over Email with Speaker

Casada's Chief Aide," *Tennessean*, May 2, 2019; Natalie Allison and Joel Ebert, "Rep. Glen Casada, Cade Cothren Sent Sexually Explicit Text Messages about Women," *Tennessean*, May 6, 2019; Joel Ebert and Natalie Allison, "House Speaker Glen Casada's Top Aide Admits Past Cocaine Use in Legislative Office Building," *Tennessean*, May 6, 2019.

68 **"I did some research and looked up."** Sergio Martínez-Beltrán, "Lawmakers Clash on Tennessee House Floor over Resolution Memorializing Teenager," WPLN News, June 16, 2020.

CHAPTER 8

96 **On Sunday, June 28, 2020.** Rebekah Hammonds, "'People's Plaza' Activists Arrested at State Capitol," NewsChannel 5, June 29, 2020.

CHAPTER 9

99 **Governor Bill Lee released a press statement.** Chas Sisk, "Tennessee Gov. Bill Lee Calls for Meeting to Consider Removal of Bust of Nathan Bedford Forrest," WPLN News, July 1, 2020.

99 **He declined even to meet with elected members.** Phil Williams, "Lee says there's reason he refused to meet with protesters, Black Caucus members," NewsChannel 5, Aug 20, 2020. https://www.newschannel5.com/news/newschannel-5-investigates/lee-says-theres-reason-he-refused-to-meet-with-protesters-black-caucus-members.

100 **In January 2019, he told reporters.** Natalie Allison, "Tennessee's Bust of Confederate Gen. Nathan Bedford Forrest Likely Isn't Going Anywhere Soon," *Tennessean*, January 2, 2019.

CHAPTER 10

117 **Until the Tennessee Historical Commission voted.** The Tennessee Historical Commission would not vote on the waiver until February 2021, per the process set forth in the Tennessee Heritage Protection Act, amended in 2016.

121 **We received a scanned, redacted packet**. Levi Ismail, "Tenn. Dept. of Safety Created Confidential Dossier of 50+ Activists during Nashville Protests," NewsChannel 5, August 9, 2021.

126 **The July 9 letter pinpointed the flaw**. Letter from Thomas H. Castelli, Stella Yarbrough, Robert Briley to Lang Wiseman, July 9, 2020.

132 **On July 29, NewsChannel 5 published a story**. Levi Ismail, "THP Pays Troopers More Than $850,000 in Overtime for June Protests and $27,000 in Travel Expenses," NewsChannel 5, July, 29, 2020.

133 **Speaker of the House Cameron Sexton released a statement**. "Gov. Lee Calls Special Session for the Tennessee General Assembly on August 10, 2020," Office of the Governor, TN.gov, August 3, 2020: https://www.tn.gov/governor/news/2020/8/3/gov--lee-calls-special-session-for-the-tennessee-general-assembly-on-august-10--2020.html.

Acknowledgments

This book would not be possible without a community of folks. I wish to express my deepest gratitude for all those who made this book a reality and breathed life into its pages through their conversations, presence, prayers, and acts of solidarity.

On October 2, 2020, when I received a Twitter message from the acquisitions editor at Vanderbilt University Press, Zachary Gresham, inviting me to write a book, I had no idea how this journey would unfold. "Do you want to write a book? I think we could publish a good one," was how he ended his message before sharing his email address. I had recently turned twenty-five years old and had neither the intention at the time nor the experience, in my mind, to write a book. It seemed like an arduous undertaking after finishing a summer of protests. I was exhausted in the deepest sense of the word. But after talking about it further with Zack, who broke the process down, and with a close friend who offered encouragement, I began writing this book as a practice of healing.

So much of who I am able to show up as in this world, before the pages of this story even began, is because of my grand-mothers. Their examples of loving, nurturing, and tending to the wounds and bruises of this world that I witnessed growing up are a continual reservoir of inspiration.

To my paternal great-grandmother, Grandma Harriet, I miss you so much and strive to live by the last advice you shared with me, "Do good and be good to yourself." I can only hope to show up as you did every day in this world. This book is dedicated to your memory.

To my maternal grandmother, Grandma Tessie (or as we say in Tagalog, Lola), you teach me in so many ways what creating spaces of sanctuary and healing looks like. Many of the pages of this book were written while sitting in your garden under the shade of the wisteria and persimmon trees or late at night at the desk of your bedroom office. Thank you for always supporting me, making sure I ate and stayed nourished throughout my season of unraveling, and for your strength throughout the Plaza on nights when I know you stayed up anxious for my safety. This book is also dedicated to you.

I want to thank Zack, my editor, for taking a chance and reaching out to me, walking with me through this entire process, offering a safe space, constant support, and generous amounts of patience. This undertaking has been over a year in the making and I am truly grateful to have an editor who was not only an expert in the craft but who also believed and participated in our movement by showing up to the Plaza that summer with his son. He reminded me about the importance of bearing witness through the written word and offered this platform to tell our story in a political environment that has often tried to erase it.

Gratitude to Vanderbilt University Press director Gianna Mosser for taking a chance on this book and truly being an ally to tell the story of our movement. I am grateful to her and the entire staff of Vanderbilt University Press for being a press rooted in academic integrity, social justice, and truth-telling—especially of the stories that the dominant narrative would rather have go untold.

As I have mentioned numerous times in vulnerability, writing this book was hard—emotionally and spiritually—and many wounds were brought to the surface. Miss Diane Nash is one of the few people I was able to share that with. I was never completely open about some of the things I experienced until writing this book. While writing was a way to expel some of those experiences from inside me, it also was retraumatizing. I am forever grateful to Miss Nash for the time she spent talking with me through some of the difficulties that were brought to the surface, and for her guidance throughout my activism journey. You told me "life is dynamic" when I felt like giving up, and I have held onto that wisdom. Thank you for being there again and again.

To Rev. William J. Barber, a prophet of our time. Thank you for taking the time out of your nonstop schedule to write the foreword for this book. It is an honor to open with your words. Ever since 2013, I have looked up to you as a model of faith and justice, from the Moral Monday protests to the Poor People's Campaign. I continue to learn from you, and I thank you for being a steadfast voice, a beloved mentor, and a spiritual father in this work. You are a civil rights giant, and I am so grateful and moved every time I see and experience your commitment to uplifting the rising generation.

To my high school English teachers, Ms. Janet Heading-ton and Ms. Karen Mason. Thank you for always empowering my writing and making me see that what I wrote mattered. More importantly, the lessons I learned in your classes go far beyond literature and the written word. You taught me about the importance of speaking up in situations of injustice, how we must connect the classroom with the world outside, and why it is necessary to balance both head and heart in all that we do.

There is a Circle of Elders that has blessed me throughout years of activism and have been there even as I face continued court dates. To Dr. Ernest "Rip" Patton, Corrine Matthews, Jane Osgerby, Ellen McPherson, Lynne McFarland, Anna Grabowski, Vivian Ervin, Tita Leny Strobel, Thenita Jones, Adrienne Latham, Dr. Charles Kimbrough, Dr. Blondell Strong, Pastor Morgan Gordy, Pastor Ken Edwards, Councilmember Zulfat Suara, and Pastor Kennard Murray—thank you for your presence in such a time as this.

Finally, my Plaza family. I love you all. This book would not have been possible without you and our experience that summer. We are connected, bonded, and you have showed me so many times what showing up for each other means as the movement continues. Niti Sharan, Ruth Reeves, Jay Terry, Dede West, Anjanette Edwards, Abby Barrentine, Megan Hurt, Rev. Venita Lewis, Steph Nikel, Ray Di Pietro, David Piñeros, Alex Kent, Sully Barrett, Gabrielle Heidrich, Xtiana, Emily, Dragon, Mohamed, Clarissa, Trayvon, Good Will, Preston, Laura, Leskia, Blaylock, Micaiah, Amber, Aaron, Macarthy, Holland, Maya, Allen, Gil, Aubrey, Miles, Mr. Kingston, Katie, Hal, Caleb, Connor, and so many others—I know our time on the Plaza meant something for each of us. We are forever changed. May each of us continue to share, process, and heal from what we overcame in the Plaza that summer, together, as we push forward in the struggle for racial justice and collective liberation.